the Hockey Dad Chronicles

An Indentured Parent's Season on the Rink

emmis books

Ed Wenck

For further information, contact the publisher at

 Emmis Books
1700 Madison Road
Cincinnati, OH 45206
www.emmisbooks.com

Library of Congress Cataloging-in-Publication Data

Wenck, Ed.
  The hockey dad chronicles / an indentured parent's season on the rink
/ by Ed Wenck.
    p. cm.
  ISBN-13: 978-1-57860-249-0
  ISBN-10: 1-57860-249-1
  1. Hockey for children. 2. Hockey--Humor. I. Title.
  GV848.6.C45W46 2005
  796.962'62--dc22

                                    2005022594

Designed by Andrea Kupper
Edited by Jessica Yerega

For Amy and Oliver

Acknowledgments

Thanks to Jim Poyser and the folks at *NUVO* for giving my writing a shot before anyone else, and thanks to Lou Harry and the crew at *Indy Men's Magazine* for all of their advice and support. Thanks to everyone at Emmis Radio in Indy for their assistance and direction—and a steady paycheck to help support my writing habit. Thanks must also be extended to Richard Hunt and Jessica Yerega at Emmis Books.

And, of course, thanks to the hockey families who grind away their winters and their bank accounts for a sport their kids truly love.

Contents

Introduction

What follows is the story, more or less, of one season of my son's youth hockey career (when he played for a team called the Indianapolis Junior Ice) and his past and future love for the game. All the names of the adults have been changed to diminish embarrassment, except the names of our coaches, who deserve all the credit one can muster for volunteering to act as the human target for all the anger and bile hurled at them by a few select parents. The names of the kids are the same—mainly so the little buggers can brag to their friends. Some of the anecdotes appeared in a weekly newspaper in Indianapolis called *NUVO*, and in a monthly publication called *Indy Men's Magazine*. Other stories were taken from notes I used on the morning radio program—*The Wank & O'Brien Show*—I co-host in that city.

I spent the bulk of one hockey season, from mid-autumn to early spring, taking notes during every hockey game, practice, or party that my son's team and the parents of the kids attended. My son and most of his teammates were ten years old during that particular season. I got the occasional ugly glance from parent and player alike when I was writing instead of cheering, but those diminished after everyone realized that the team's exploits were being immortalized in ink on cheap newsprint.

The sport of ice hockey is going through a transitional period as I write this. Professional hockey, especially at the American major league levels, has suffered crippling losses in popularity and revenue as a result of labor/management squabbles and declining TV viewership—even as the sport seems to be growing overseas.

The status of ice hockey in Indianapolis may well hold the key to the sport's rebirth on the rest of the continent: Our low-level pro team is gone, only to be replaced by a top-tier amateur team. Now fans of the sport in Indy can watch kids ages sixteen to twenty, recruited from all over North America, as those kids try to impress scouts from big league teams and NCAA Division I hockey schools alike. I truly hope the experiment works.

WARM-UP

When my son, Oliver, was just a diapered toddler, his Aunt Kathleen gave him a small plastic hockey stick. I figure the stick cost Kathleen about six bucks.

At last count, I figure that stick has probably cost my family about thirty thousand dollars.

I'm not saying that it was the stick and the stick alone that fostered my boy's interest in the Sport of the Frozen Pond (and all the bloody time and money that went along with said interest). I am, however, willing to lay the blame squarely at somebody else's feet.

Okay, so my wife and I were complicit. We were not without blame. We took the kid to his first hockey game.

It took place in Johnstown, Pennsylvania, at a creaking, rusty old airplane hangar of a rink called the Johnstown War Memorial. The venue sat maybe three thousand, and it was packed for each and every game. My son was about three at the time.

The local squad, originally called the Johnstown Jets, had been the inspiration for the Charlestown Chiefs, the fictional team in the movie *Slap Shot*. The Jets had disbanded, and when hockey returned to Johnstown, the franchise had chosen the nickname "Chiefs" to honor the film in return. (The Chiefs' style of play mirrored the film quite a bit, too—fighting was so common the locals decided to sit a priest next to the penalty box so that everybody on the team made it to confession.) A good bit of the film had been shot inside the War Memorial—as well as some incredibly depressing exterior footage. Johnstown was a steel town, not a vacation spot.

Oliver was thrilled by the Chiefs. He clapped when they scored. He clapped when they skated. He clapped when they checked. He clapped when they fought. He clapped for the Zamboni, the machine that smoothed the ice between periods.

On his next birthday, after witnessing his very first hockey game, my son received that little plastic hockey stick from his Aunt Kathy.

Oliver immediately set about turning our kitchen floor into an ersatz hockey rink. He'd hammer dents into the linoleum with the blade of the stick as his stockinged feet slid back and forth. (We lost a big chunk of our security deposit when we moved out of that apartment—our landlord took one look at the kitchen floor and asked: "What did you people *do*?") Cooking became painful—standing at the stove meant you had your back turned to the game, and an errant puck often made contact with the Achilles tendon of the poor slob playing chef at that moment.

I said "puck." Ha. "Puck" was whatever Oliver could smack with a stick. Loose change, golf balls, you name it—Oliver would use anything and everything that could possibly bruise Mom and Dad's legs. We finally bought the child two dozen foam-rubber balls when his horrified mother walked into the kitchen only to find the kid winding up to take a swipe at a shot glass. He'd climbed on the counter and taken the glass from a cupboard after everything else he'd been shooting wound up under the oven.

My wife called up Aunt Kathleen and asked her if she intended to have kids. My wife told Kathleen that if Kath ever bore children, my wife would outfit the little buggers with throwing knives.

Oliver made crowd noises, buzzer noises, whistles, catcalls, cheers, and boos. He'd play, stop, drag a stool to the edge of the linoleum, and sit down. He'd tell us that the man in the striped shirt had put him in "time-out."

One day we saw our boy pushing his little stool back and forth across the tile and making a motorboat noise.

"What are you doing?" asked my wife.

"Making Zamboni!" replied the kid.

For the next two years the boy made Zamboni. And for the next two years the boy asked if he could play hockey. He wanted jerseys and sticks for Christmas, skates and pads for his birthday. He begged us to take him out to the local rink. He'd grab the top of an orange safety cone and use it like an old man uses a walker, staggering after it with both hands on the point of the cone until his feet began to glide intuitively. My wife and I thought that this would satisfy the child for a year or two longer, mastering the skates before he took the next awful step. It would've, too—if it hadn't been for that bastard Emilio Estevez.

Yeah, I'm really gonna spread this blame around.

Emilio Estevez played the role of the reluctant hockey coach in a shlocky Disney film called *The Mighty Ducks*. (Are you picking up the fact that my family watches a whole helluva lot of old sports movies?) He played the role again in *D2* (Disney shorthand for *The Mighty Ducks Part 2*), and made a cameo in *D3*. My son thought Emilio Estevez was the coolest guy in the world. My son wanted to play hockey for Emilio Estevez.

Why? Well, simple! Emilio Estevez took a rag-tag bunch of misfits and turned them into a winning hockey team! Emilio Estevez discovered that his old nemesis was coaching the very team that the Mighty Ducks had to beat to win it all! Emilio Estevez could've voiced the dialogue for this movie in his sleep, it was so freakin' predictable!

On the first day that my son went to practice hockey with his very first team, long before standard equipment had been issued by the league, I looked around at the other parents unpacking their sons' and daughters' equipment bags. Each and every last one pulled out a practice jersey that featured a cartoon image of a waterfowl and block green typeface that read "Mighty Ducks."

The parents exchanged glances, made eye contact. We all knew what had passed between us. We had all made the same unspoken pact. Should any one of us ever happen to encounter Emilio Estevez, it was now our solemn obligation to kill him.

Aunt Kathleen? She was family. I had to let her live.

Emilio Estevez and the Walt Disney Company had sealed the deal; they were the final part of the unholy trinity that turned me, my wife, and our lone offspring into the winter gypsies known as a "travel hockey family." Broken down into different squads by age and skill level, travel hockey teams can log hundreds of miles every weekend as the kids match up against squads of similar age and ability. By the time my boy had turned a decade old, we had joined the Indianapolis Junior Ice Squirt "A" (better than "B," not quick enough to be classified "AA") Travel Hockey squad. "Squirt" means too old for the "Mite" division but too young for the "Pee Wee" division; all the kids were roughly nine to ten years of age.

My ten-year-old son now *really* sat in the box when the man in the striped shirt put him in time-out. My son, Oliver, wearing the number seventy-four on his back, was a defenseman for a youth hockey team that spent two weekends a month on the road in towns all over the Midwest. The remaining weekends were occupied with home games in various rinks around Indianapolis. The average Saturday schedule? Play one, rest for an hour, play a second game—then do it all over again on Sunday.

Yep, that's right—two hockey games in a day, sometimes two in a single afternoon. Why? If you're traveling to a city in another state and ice time is at a premium, then the logistics of league play overshadow your child's exhaustion. Hockey moms and dads may be broke, but they're usually wearing a silly and romantic grin— travel hockey kids sleep a *lot*.

Travel hockey kids—exhausted, bruised, and abused, lugging bags of gear all over the map, sleeping sitting up in the backseat of the car only to wind up at some decrepit rink in Dayton or Saginaw, then dressing in damp, clammy, stinking equipment that never seems to dry—and what's their payoff, their sweet reward? They take to the ice at seven o'clock on a Saturday morning while their classmates are chewing their way through bowls of Cap'n Crunch and blocks of Nicktoons. Alas, there's no sugary cereal or SpongeBob for the travel hockey kids; the travel hockey kids are skating, skating, surrounded by the deafening roar of the odd mom or dad who is Way Too Into It, their shouts ringing off the metal and fiberglass that wraps around a pad of ice, brutally hard and cold.

They love it. Travel kids are the ones with the greatest inexplicable love for the sport of hockey.

Hockey. What the hell was hockey? I could barely skate myself. I had always dreamt of teaching my son everything I knew about the sport of football, the game I loved. The finesse and raw power of pigskin—that was a sport I understood. I was five-foot-nine-inches, 150 pounds dripping wet. I had always been too small and slight for football. My son was burly and tall for his age. Too slow to be a linebacker, maybe, but perfectly built to be an old-school pocket-passing quarterback.

No matter. My ten-year-old played hockey. My ten-year-old loved hockey. My wife and I didn't pick this sport. The kid did.

C'mon—what parent in his right mind would ever pick hockey for his child?

The sport is violent and aggressive. You're strapping knives on a kid's feet, hurling a hard rubber disc at him, and telling him to smack it with a club. Later, you'll tell him to throw his body at other bodies all skating at top speed on that hard, cold surface, occasionally flying headlong into a barely forgiving wall that rings the rink, a wall topped by a clear sheet of plastic that allows the spectator to witness his child's agony from mere inches away.

Why would anyone volunteer her little miracle for this madness? Anytime hockey makes the front pages of the papers, the story has nothing to do with talent or records or the thrill of victory or the agony of defeat. Hockey news has been about lockouts and lawsuits and bickering and, ultimately, violence. (During the last labor stoppage, a satirical e-mail was passed around among fans of the sport urging ticket-holders to help their local poor, downtrodden NHL players through their personal fiscal crises. Part of the text went something like: "For the cost of only $720 a day—less than a big-screen TV—you can ensure that an NHL player will golf in Aruba instead of Florida this year. Won't you please help?")

And then there's the inevitable thuggery. Guys get hurt in other sports, sure—but the delivery of bodily harm to another human is never as blatantly intentional as it is in the sport of ice hockey. Hell, fighting—the actual stoppage of a game for the exchange of punches—is an accepted and expected part of the sport at the professional level. Fights that occur on the field of play during most sports automatically lead to player ejections. Fighting in professional hockey is punished with five minutes of rest.

Then there's the financial cost.

Ice time—the basic fee for a season that starts in October and runs through March—averages about $250 a month. Gear is another thing—skates, shin guards, cup, sock support, padded pants, chest protector, elbow and arm pads, gloves, neck guard, helmet, mouth guard, skates, and stick—buy it used and you're looking at an absolute minimum of three hundred bills. Most parents shell out two or three times that amount to guarantee safety. You'll also need a hundred-dollar hockey bag to haul that junk around.

Jerseys and socks are often included in the fees, but there are other goodies that the team manager doesn't mention at the start of the season. Matching pants, mock turtlenecks, and pullovers for the kids to wear during the journeys to and from the rink. Team photos, a solo eight-by-ten or five-by-seven with some wallet-size numbers for the grandparents. Plaques. Fundraising items. Team sweatshirts and caps for Mom and Dad to wear in the bleachers.

You're not done. A kid in travel hockey plays from two to four games per week, many in cities far enough away from home to require a hotel stay. Sometimes the parents will rent a bus for single-day trips, but usually everybody drives themselves. Mix in two or three practices a week, gas, and food, and you've got a time/cash outlay of staggering proportions. The total monthly tab for our ten-year-old son's hockey career ran much higher than our monthly grocery bill.

In the season before his advancement to the Squirt bracket, my son had played in the Mite division at an All-Star level (a notch below full-blown travel hockey). Still, we did visit teams in other cities. I'd guess that I easily shelled out a total of four thousand bucks for the entire season. At the end of the year, my son received a stylish gunmetal trophy approximately six inches high. I figured the retail value on the trophy came in at roughly $14.99.

I've heard parents of children who play travel baseball or soccer complain about the cost. I've heard the hoopster moms and dads express concern about the price of basketball shoes. When Oliver decided to add lacrosse as another participatory sport at the age of eleven, his coach addressed an introductory meeting of the parents with an apology:

"I hate to tell you this, but the fees for the season have gone up since I spoke with most of you."

I held my breath.

"Instead of $200, we have to ask you for $225."

Two hundred twenty five bucks? FOR THE WHOLE FREAKING SEASON?

I could barely contain my glee. I tried to get the other parents to do the wave. Carry the coach on our shoulders. Dump a Gatorade bucket on the guy. The other hockey parents were right there with me. The Little League moms and dads glared. An entire season of lacrosse, in case you're keeping score, came in under the price of a single month of ice hockey.

I shelled out. I paid up. My boy was my boy alone, an only child, the apple of my eye. We sent the kid to private school, a Montessori school. I called the boy's education "my Saab convertible." I drove a leased Saturn sedan instead of a sexy Swedish ride.

I referred to my son's hockey career as "my big-screen TV." The family still watched the RCA tube we'd bought in the late '80s.

No matter. My kid played hockey. My kid loved hockey.

Hockey. What the hell was hockey?

The rules are as follows: Put the puck in the net. Stay out of the penalty box. Watch the blue lines. Don't run it offsides. Don't ice it unless you're a man down from a penalty. If you're not following this, don't worry—the kid's been in it for years now and I'm still catching up.

There are five players skating free, unless you're short because someone's in the box. Three play offense, two play defense, and one poor, nervous kid crouches in the goal. (The parents of the kid in the net paid three times what you did for all that crap the goalie's wearing to keep from getting killed. Buy them lunch.)

Substitutions occur regularly. When your kid's taking a break, yell, "Good shift!" When your kid's been benched, don't yell at the coach. Okay, okay, you shelled out all that money, drove two hundred miles and ate one more Egg McSomething for breakfast just so junior can spend the entire game on his ass. You want to yell at the coach. Your kid was sick, he was tired, he was lazy, he was just being a ten-year-old. The coach sat him. The coach is trying to win. The other parents want the team to win. Some want it badly. When the kids lose, *everybody* yells at the coach.

Recently a litigious lunkhead (Canadian, not a U.S. citizen this time, thank God) decided to sue his son's hockey league over the fact that his little Lemieux wasn't handed the MVP trophy for the season. The award had apparently gone to someone who had scored fewer goals over the course of the year than the plaintiff's kid. I didn't follow the case—I don't even know if it made it to court—but the league surely cited other mitigating circumstances: the winner was better at defense, scored at more critical moments, had less of a jerk for a dad, and so on. The action of a lawsuit was extreme, but the attitude is common.

Junior sat, junior lost the hockey Heisman, junior bore the brunt of a terrible call. Despite all the money and sweat and tire rubber you've poured into this sport, your kid is still not the very, very best. You can yell, you can scream, you can sue—but just for a second, put your wallet away. Swallow your pride. Look at those little buggers out there on the ice.

The aforementioned lunkhead has clearly forgotten the joy of the thing. It's great to watch the kids play. It's a chance to meet other parents from damn near every walk of life. And we all— every hockey mom and pop—carry a secret. The hidden benefit. The silent pro to every con.

Hockey is the greatest excuse in the world.

Want to bail on a business dinner or a night out with some depressed downsized co-worker? There's always a skating clinic someplace! Feel like spending the holidays close to home? Junior's playing the weekend after Turkey Day! Yard work? Housecleaning? No way—the kid has a doubleheader in Louisville that starts just after dawn!

(Personally, I enjoy a scaled-back Thanksgiving amidst all this incessant stickin'. My wife always strives to make the harvest feast a monumental event. She has obsessed over Bird Thursday to the point where she's trying to duplicate menu items served at the original meal. I'm not kidding. Next year we're having venison and smallpox.)

Ahh, hockey, the liberator! The sporting emancipator! Can you think of a more noble excuse for skipping church than cheering on junior from beside a rink? Is there a better reason to lock up the house and spend the night in the lobby of a strange hotel, eating pizza and drinking beer with your family, friends, and compatriots?

Before you sue, before you start screaming at the refs, the coach, or the parents on the other team (hell, the parents on your team), remember the get-out-of-anything-free card that the puck provides the parent.

Oh, yeah, and there's another thing.

The hockey economy.

Not the gear, not the rink fees, not the part-time cash for the Zamboni driver. The hockey economy answers the question: Can you possibly come up with any reason why a town like Fort Wayne, Indiana, makes a single nickel in *tourism?*

Danville, Illinois! Toledo, Ohio! Sometimes the Greyhound breaks down in these towns, maybe—but have any of these places ever been actual *destinations?*

Travel hockey makes them viable attractions in their own right! Travel hockey brings new blood into the Pizza Huts and Applebees! Travel hockey fills the hotel rooms in the dead of winter when the migrant workers have gone home to *su casa!* Travel hockey draws gas from the pumps at the Shell station and chews up the "weekend anywhere minutes" on the cellular contract!

Dayton or Muncie or Decatur—who cares? Every Courtyard by Marriott looks the same: heated pool, breakfast buffet, almost-dirty movies available on pay-per-view. Buy some beer and a bag of Taco Bell! The kids are all asleep, dreaming of their big game against the Storm or the Cyclones or the River Lemurs or whoever the hell it is they're playing tomorrow, while the parents sit out in the hall, drinking rum-and-Cokes and trading filthy stories and mindless gossip.

Take all of what I've said and blend it, mix it together, then consider:

The Hockey dad is the luckiest man alive.

No parent in his right mind would pick hockey for his child.

Ergo—the kid picked the sport, no guilt for you.

Hockey is the greatest excuse in the world.

Ergo—you get to blow off church to spend time at a sporting

event, no guilt for you.

Hockey requires traveling to America's suburbs and shopping malls.

Ergo—you get to eat nachos every weekend, no guilt for you.

Hockey boosts the economies of some towns that could really use it.

Ergo—the cardiac event from all those nachos is a patriotic sacrifice, no guilt for you.

Now the kicker: All the nachos and cheering, all the missed Masses and vespers—*you did it to spend time with the family.*

The best dads spend time with the family. Your time with the family involves garbage food and spectator sports. You are truly blessed, my friend. You are truly blessed.

Hockey. What the hell was hockey?

FACE-OFF

The first year my son played organized hockey he skated for a team called The Ducks (KILL EMILIO KILL EMILIO KILL EMILIO) in the "Mini-Mite" division of the Pepsi Coliseum league. (Mini-Mites are the youngest kids allowed to play; some are only four when they start.) The Pepsi Coliseum was—and is—an ancient cavern that sat across from a horse track on the Indiana State Fairgrounds on 38th Street in Indianapolis, on the edge of an economically depressed part of town. Anybody who wanted to buy crack during practice would've had to travel only a block or two to get a bag.

The fairgrounds seemed to exist in another universe—long buildings dedicated to housing livestock for two weeks every year, then hosting corn conventions and flea markets for the rest of the calendar. The fairgrounds played host to some of the biggest country music acts to visit the city. Until the practice was outlawed, men who belonged to the Nation of Islam tried to raise money for Minister Farrakhan just outside the fairground gates by selling pecan pies and newspapers.

The Coliseum was built in 1939 for the hefty sum of one million bucks. The first event at the place was a sold-out hockey game: Indy's franchise beat the Syracuse Stars on a rink that's still substantially larger than today's standard professional surface. (The pros play on a rink that's 200 feet long by 85 wide; the Coliseum is 215 by 90 to allow enough room for a state fair horse show on the same surface. It might not seem like a big difference—until your six-year-old rookie skater spends an hour on a Saturday afternoon chasing a puck across that frozen pond. After the game, he'll fall asleep on the ride home and won't wake up until church on Sunday.)

The Coliseum is where the Beatles made their debut in the Hoosier State. We have in our home two old photographs of that event. In one, the Fab Four surround Miss Indiana State Fair 1964. Miss Indiana State Fair 1964 is beaming back at the crowd in front of her. She's a blonde girl about the same height as the fellas, and she seems to be especially attracted to John. In fact, she seems to be trying to back into John in order to somehow climb into his suit with him. Paul is smirking at John, Ringo is smirking at George, George seems to be looking at Miss Indiana State Fair 1964's chest, and John Lennon appears stoned—just waitin' for Yoko.

In the other picture, the photographer had set up shop just behind the Beatles off to stage left. A gauntlet of state troopers rings the stage, looking to see if any of the screaming teenage girls in the crowd appear ready to make a run for the stage and crawl into John Lennon's suit.

The most remarkable thing about both photographs? The Coliseum looks exactly the same now as it did in 1964.

The Coliseum played host to a speech by a Presidential hopeful named John F. Kennedy in 1959. Shortly after the attacks of September 11, 2001, the Coliseum was the setting for a speech by

President George W. Bush. The Coliseum was where Indy's pro hoops team, the Pacers, saw seasons that won ABA Championships. (The fairgrounds gave The Pacers their name—the team's handle was a nod to the horse track just across the street. The track was a course used primarily by trotters, horses that carried their riders in low-slung buggies behind the animals.)

A few years back, the Coliseum saw a six-figure renovation. The old wooden seats were torn out and replaced with brilliant blue plastic numbers that cradled a spectator's posterior in comfort. The building's interior picked up a fresh coat of paint and a JumboTron at one end of the building. The local hockey franchise started selling Canadian beer at the concession stands. The skate shop was scrubbed and given a new neon sign—you could buy tape and pucks and overpriced skates in a brighter environment. The old Zamboni was even replaced by a snappy new two-tone model that chugged along with half the sound and one-quarter the smoke of the old creaking ice-cutter.

It didn't matter. The Coliseum was still a dump.

The Coliseum was dank and vile and always stank of diesel fuel and greasy hot dogs. An art-deco-style place, the Coliseum was still, despite the face-lift, fronted by perhaps two dozen metal and glass doors, all painted a grisly shade of mint green that might've been popular for thirty minutes at some point during Kennedy's speech. No matter how fresh the paint was or how new the seats were, the Coliseum remained dark and downright creepy. My wife always said the place gave her the chills. Maybe her discomfort was a bit of leftover psychic energy.

In 1963, a year before the Beatles showed up in Indiana, the Coliseum suffered a tragedy that garnered national headlines from coast to coast. On Halloween night just after eleven o'clock, during opening night of a show called "Holiday on

Ice," a propane tank that supplied flame for a popcorn popper began to leak. A stray spark ignited the gas, and the tank, sitting directly underneath a section of bleachers, exploded with a force violent enough to send bodies flying sixty feet into the air. As the survivors tried to flee the collapsing stands, a second explosion ripped through the crowd. The blasts claimed seventy-four lives and injured four hundred. The Coliseum was closed for repairs until the Beatles came to play the following year.

The story was—and is—the greatest single disaster ever to occur in the city of Indianapolis. On milestone anniversaries of the event, the local TV news organizations assemble flashback stories to remind everyone of the gruesome details surrounding the explosion. When Oliver began to play at the Coliseum, we were unaware of the history, my wife and I both being of East Coast extraction. After she heard about the blast, my wife's feelings about the rink went from a bad vibe to outright fear. She dreaded having to haul Ollie to the Pepsi Coliseum by herself.

In truth, I felt the same way about the place. Everything about the Coliseum was just a little—off. The acoustics were lousy. The building was loaded with cold spots, hot spots—no one area of the building ever seemed to be the right temperature. Rows of battered old picnic tables sat behind the glass at one end of the rink so that you could eat the pizzas you'd ordered after the game in relative comfort—until you realized you'd picked up seven or eight splinters in the butt.

Even the locker rooms were odd. They sat underneath the stands in cramped crawlspaces that forced anybody taller than four-foot-eleven to duck constantly while trying to help get her child dressed for a game. Any absent-minded attempt to stand up straight resulted in cracking one's head against the stepped concrete ceiling. You could always tell when a team from out of town had played its first game at the Coliseum—at least three parents would leave the rink rubbing the egg-shaped knots on their foreheads. Dodging the mice that skittered through the locker rooms also led to more than one mild concussion. More than one little rodent had hitched a ride out of the Coliseum in some random kid's hockey bag only to be discovered by a terrified, shrieking hockey mom who was preparing to wash junior's socks and jerseys.

The Coliseum had been the venue for hockey in Indy since it had opened in '39, but the '63 explosion drove the pro team, the Indy Capitols, to look for accommodations elsewhere. The Caps wound up in Cincinnati, and hockey in Indy wound up finding a home in Market Square Arena, the building that saw the professional debut of Number 99, the Great One, Wayne Gretzky. His first pro game was with a team called the Indianapolis Racers.

The banner now hangs in the Coliseum: GRETZKY 99. It was moved there when Market Square Arena ceased to exist. MSA was professionally imploded in 2001, and the Indianapolis Ice, the pro hockey team founded in 1988, began to split its time between the Coliseum and Conseco Fieldhouse. (The pro-Ice have since disbanded, replaced by the amateur development squad called The Indiana Ice.)

My son's first games in that soda pop cavern off of 38th Street looked like ice-bound rugby scrums. Imagine ten kids in oversized jerseys staggering around on skates in a perpetual circle, flailing away at a puck that emerged from the crowd only two or three times per match to dribble into a goal. The kids would congregate in a "swarm" (in fact, some coaches of both hockey and soccer at this level have drawn up plays called "swarm right" and "swarm left") and hack away at the disc in the middle of the knot like a gang of cavemen trying to bring down a wooly mammoth with their clubs.

Worse, the children's skating style at this level resembled a drunken ballerina attempting to walk on point. The tips of the kids' skates dug into the ice, propelling them headlong for a few steps before they settled into the notion of actually gliding on their blades. As the swarm charged back and forth across the rink, one or two stragglers who hadn't quite gotten the whole skating thing together would trot after the huddle, never making contact with puck or opposing player, just desperately trying to follow the action.

The littlest skaters, the kids just five and six years old and making their first valiant efforts to figure out the game, are the very living definition of determination. Drowning in pads and pants and gloves and a helmet that makes the child so top-heavy he looks like he may keel over from the sheer weight of the thing, these little atheletes trudge back and forth like ants upon the giant ancient glacier that cut Lake Michigan itself. Their jaws are set, their eyes are steely, the Star Wars pajama tops below their pads are soaked in the sweat of grim competition. They do not need their mommies, they do not need their daddies, they are venturing forth without the simple comfort of their binkies or their blankies or their Beanie Babies, driving toward the puck at a steady two-and-a-half miles per hour until, upon reaching said rubber disc, they manage to jam their stick into the ice at such an angle that the twig stops short— and the kids immediately knock the wind out of themselves with the butt end of the thing.

The better skaters learn early on how to add NOISE and DRAMA to the game. NOISE is easy—smack your stick against the Plexiglas that separates player from spectator! Run into the boards, chest thrust forward, and BANG! All that padding absorbs the shock and you emerge uninjured from what appeared to Mom to be a collision one step removed from a freeway accident.

DRAMA is a bit more labor intensive. DRAMA usually

occurs when your tiptoe-start doesn't result in a smooth glide, but rather in a face-plant into the surface of the ice. DRAMA includes rolling about on the ice, moaning and wailing and rending one's jersey, threatening to peel the very face of a Mighty Duck (KILL EMILIO KILL EMILIO KILL EMILIO) from the front of your sweater. This maneuver is often coupled with the pointing of an accusatory glove toward an enemy team member, claiming you'd been pushed as you roll your head back and forth on the frozen pond, your noodle safe and snug in your padded soup tureen of a helmet.

Kids who master DRAMA seldom last for more than a season or two of organized ice hockey. The ones who master NOISE are destined to play for many years. Some of those same noisemakers my boy skated with on the Ducks team became traveling players on the Junior Ice.

A lot of those kids skated with or against my son in the years between. We watched them all develop their game together. They added skills every year: skating backwards, passing, positioning on the ice, celebrating properly after a goal. (Actually, they mastered the celebration thing right off the bat. One knee up, stick in the air, suffocate the kid who just scored by piling on him all at once.)

They also learned how to shoot around a real, live, honest-to-God goalie.

At the beginner levels of youth hockey, an orange cone is placed in the goal. This simple traffic device is an excellent substitute for an actual person when six-year-olds are attempting to put the puck into the net. Watching a six-year-old attempting to string together the varied tasks of skating, handling a stick, putting the stick on the puck, and causing said puck to travel forward into a goal is a little like watching a bird trying to build a nest in the lead car of a moving rollercoaster.

At some point, most parents of Mini-Mite players ask aloud why the orange cone hasn't been signed by the Detroit Red Wings. The damn cone stops *everything*.

About the same time that a living, breathing human goalie is added to the mix, expensive pads and all, the many tasks involved in skating and shooting seem to merge into a graceful flow. Pretty soon, youth hockey takes on the look of a very slow square dance punctuated with the occasional breakaway goal or accidental trip.

Until, of course, you introduce the notion of "changing on the fly." This is, simply put, the substitution of one player for another without a stoppage in play. At the beginner levels, the clock is stopped every two minutes during a ten-minute period so that a new batch of players can leave the bench and take their positions on the ice. When the kids start playing twelve-minute periods, then the offensive or defensive groups of players on the ice—"lines"—will skate over to the bench while their replacements skate into the flow of the play.

If the children are using the doors at either end of the bench, a line change can be a fairly smooth and only occasionally harrowing event. (*Harrowing* comes when all five players on your team decide to take a break while all five of the other side's skaters are crowded around *your* goalie. This usually happens only once, and either the kids are scared into never repeating the mistake or your son's coach's head explodes and your team has to forfeit the season.) It's when the children try to mimic the pros that problems erupt.

Professional hockey players and mostly-grown amateurs don't line up at a door to exit the bench. They simply hop over the boards in front of the bench. This is an effective and efficient way to enter the arena of play—if you're five-foot-six or better. If you're still too small to ride the Tilt-A-Whirl at the state fair, then attempting this technique is going to make you look like one of the dumber perps on the TV show *COPS*: hung up on a chain-link fence with the money from the liquor store you just robbed falling from your pockets, and The Man is coming up quick.

More than once I've seen a child successfully navigate the steeplechase obstacle between bench and ice only to have the back of his jersey catch on a hinge or a snag or a stray piece of busted hockey rink. The child's feet will be flailing away at top speed while he stares at his teammates with a look of utter bewilderment—*why ain't I movin'?*

Eventually, though, the kids get it—the game comes together. They've got the ability to walk, chew gum, rub their stomachs, and pat their heads all at once. They exit the bench smoothly and skate quickly into position, both hands on their sticks, blades against the ice as they travel with the flow of the game. I could see Oliver assembling all the fundamental parts of an ice hockey match in his head:

*Cover the guy who wants to shoot at my goalie—he's in front of our net, waiting for a pass—keep the game in front of you—wait, we've got the puck! We're moving it away from our net! We're on a break! Follow the play! Position! Stop just inside the blue line now that we're down at their end of the ice! Keep the puck in this zone! Slap your stick against the ice—let the offensive guys know you're open for a pass! The puck is mine! The puck is mine! I'm going to shoot the—*AWW GEEZ THAT KID FROM TOLEDO JUST STOLE THE PUCK AWAY FROM ME, AND HE'S ALL BY HIMSELF ON A BREAKAWAY SO I GUESS I'LL TRIP HIM AND SPEND TWO MINUTES IN THE BOX ...

The kids who played with Oliver on the Junior Ice Squirt A travel team were at this stage when the final element was added. They'd learned finesse and technique. And then, on a warm November day in Danville, Illinois, the last transformation began.

The kids started hitting.

NOVEMBER—1ˢᵗ Period

It was fitting, I think, that the hitting started in Danville.

Danville lies about an hour south of Chicago just west of the Indiana border. Danville "Welcomes You to Illinois!" Danville is "The Home of Dick and Jerry—the Van Dyke Brothers!" Danville is "Where Gene Hackman Was Born!" They tell you this stuff on the "Now Entering Danville" signs.

They don't mention that Danville is the mullet capital of the Midwest.

[**MULLET**, *n*: 1) a hairstyle popularized in the early 1980s that features a short cut on the front and top of the skull with much longer growth in the back, making the wearer's head take on the aerodynamic shape of a 1979 Trans Am; 2) hockey hair.]

Not Kalamazoo, Michigan, not Fort Wayne, Indiana, hell, not even the citizens of Toledo, Ohio, can match the business-up-front-party-in-the-back-Foreigner-STILL-rocks look that the ladies and gents are sportin' in Danville. These folks—and their kids—have the haircuts that announce:

"It's time to play some HOCKEY, dammit!"

On a Saturday morn late in the fall, as I stood in the stands of a Danville rink waiting for the Indianapolis Junior Ice Squirt A Travel Hockey team to emerge from the locker room, I stared in awe at the near-perfect mullet owned by the gent driving the Zamboni around the ice. Wearing a T-shirt that announced his fondness for the worm at the bottom of a bottle of mescal, the dude looked like the kind of person who truly believed that the End of All Good Music coincided with the death of Led Zeppelin's drummer. While he shaved and smoothed the ice under fluorescent lights surrounded by a sea of nearly-empty orange plastic seats above the boards and glass, I noticed that the guy had a tattoo on his neck.

A tattoo.

On his neck.

If ever an adornment of the human body could announce to the viewer: "Don't mess with me, jackass," it surely must be the neck tattoo. Is there any possible situation in which it's prudent to argue with a guy who's willing to have an electrified needle etch a design *directly on top of his jugular vein?*

The look—the chained wallet, the mullet, the T-shirt—extended to the parents of the Danville kids. As far as any of these folks were concerned, clean Levi's were church-goin' pant, and the local radio station better play at least one AC/DC song per hour or the citizenry would start phoning in death threats on the request line. The town's richest purveyor of ladies' fashions had to be the guy who sold leather blazers.

It was fitting, I think, that the hitting started in Danville.

The second game we played on that Saturday morning in that Illinois town was a watershed event, a turning point in the year. A season of grace became a season of puck. Hockey became "HOCKEY, dammit!"

In Little League baseball, a collision is an accident. In Pop

Warner football, a collision is part of the game from Day One. In youth hockey, the hits are introduced slowly. The Squirts are allowed to thump each other a bit, but when the kids attain the next level, Pee Wee, checking is allowed.

The league didn't yet allow checking, but the rules regarding "incidental contact" became a lot tougher to decipher on that day in Danville. (Depending on the refs in any given city or, for that matter, at any given rink, the games could run the gamut from an exercise in finesse and passing to the final ten minutes of the movie *Slap Shot*.) During the first matchup, the refs in Danville let the kids make contact—for the most part. Some kids wanted to put a body on a body. Some kids wanted to dodge the other madmen out there on the ice at any and all costs. Some kids started jawing at the refs as much as the parents and the coaches. Some kids who were normally as quiet as church mice started spending time in the penalty box.

During the second game in Danville, we saw the refs allow full-on, full-speed, shoulder-meets-sternum checking, and the referees were loath to hit the whistle and call a penalty for "checking in a non-checking league." Maybe they were scared that the Indy parents were as tough as the local moms and dads. Better not whistle *anyone* for an infraction no matter what jersey the kid has on, eh?

Eventually, of course, the refs had to blow the whistle. It was a non-checking league. Some parent somewhere was bound to complain about Squirts driving other Squirts into the boards, into the ice, into each other …

When the hitting started, the parents underwent a change themselves. Blood began to boil and bile began to rise. Some of the hockey parents thought the playing field wasn't level. The refs were calling *our* kids for hitting, not *their* kids. *Our* kids were being treated unfairly. *Our* kids, whom we loved and adored and cherished and had driven to this god-forsaken town at seven o'clock on a Saturday morning after spending all this money on … well, you get the point.

Halfway through the second period of the second game, one of the two striped shirts on the ice decided that the officials were losing control of the game. He raised his arm and whistled a penalty. One of Oliver's best friends on the team, a kid named Taylor but known to everyone as "Taz," was flagged for a hit. Two minutes in the box.

A few Indy parents booed. At the ref, not the kid.

Halfway through Taz's penalty, a kid from Danville was whistled for a "bench minor" penalty—two minutes in the box to think about what he'd done—for checking in a non-checking league.

All the Danville parents booed. Again, at the ref.

Parents were getting very cranky. Coaches were getting very cranky. The refs wanted to leave the ice in a hurry at the end of the third period.

I was becoming amazed at how un-conflicted some parents seemed. They saw nothing wrong with hurling obscenities at child, coach, or referee. They saw nothing wrong with displaying an absolute lack of self-control in front of their impressionable little pre-adolescent winger.

I also became amazed at how much I was yelling.

I had managed to hold off on the insults (although the temptation to repeat a gem like "Get yer head outta yer ass, ref, yer missing a good hockey game!" was pretty powerful). Nonetheless, I was interjecting a fair share of "Aww, c'mon!" and "Terrible call!" commentary at some pretty intense sound-pressure levels.

I noticed that the coaches were yelling, too.

A coach that Oliver had in later years—when he started hitting legally in the next age bracket—told me what his strategy was for a good heckle directed at the ref. Coach Tom gave me the fine points:

"If you call a ref an idiot, he might flag the coach who's calling him out and put one of your guys in the box (hockey's version of the technical foul in basketball). Y'know what I do? I yell 'That call was BRUTAL!' The ref knows you're pissed, but you didn't tell him the call stunk out loud. It's not a judgment about the ref's intelligence or whether or not he's playing fair—get it?"

Got it. Coaches can yell, but only parents can actually form *insults*.

The down time between periods gave me time to reflect. Was anybody privately embarrassed by all their histrionics? I was.

I needed to remind myself that those players out there skating past the blue lines weren't men and women, they were kids, and therefore—by definition—they were still playing a kids' game.

It was a kids' game. *Rugrats* T-shirts lurked beneath their chest protectors.

It was a kids' game. Stick, puck, and net were on equal footing in the ten-year-old universe with LEGOs, Hot Wheels, and a four-hour block of *Hey Arnold!* on Nickelodeon.

It was a kids' game. You could tell by the nicknames the moms still carried for the li'l buggers on the ice.

Sure, the kids would tell you that their names were Slayer and Taz and Shred and Crazy-Eyes Pasty Killa, but the 'rents in the stands knew the truth: Those little thugs had names like Num-Nums and Pookie. (You wanna see real tears? Out Pookie in the locker room.)

Time-Out: ACTUAL DIALOGUE OVERHEARD IN THE LOCKER ROOM PROVING THAT IT'S STILL A KIDS' GAME

"Spider-Man could kick Batman's butt anytime, anywhere!"

"My mom checks under my jacket every day to see if I'm saggin'!"

"Batman doesn't have any super powers or anything!"

"I found a whole buncha gum in the penalty box!"

"My mom threw away my Ludacris CD!"

"Batman would still be a good goalie if he used his cape!"

"That guy who invented SpongeBob doesn't even draw SpongeBob any more!"

"Spider-Man would be the best goalie 'cause of his webbing!"

"My mom threw away my Eminem CD and my Busta Rhymes CD!"

"Yeah? Once I found three Twizzlers and an Ace of Spades with a naked lady on it in the penalty box!"

J

NOVEMBER—2ⁿᵈ Period

Toward the end of the Danville game, with our kids up by a comfortable three-goal margin, I wandered out of the stands and peered through a gap in the Plexiglas above the boards. The acoustics in most rinks are abysmal—quiet sounds are muffled, loud sounds are amplified in a horrible, ringing crescendo—but for some reason, I could hear the kids on the ice as they skated past me in the Danville rink.

At that moment I realized something profound. These kids weren't training to be hockey players. They were training to be play-by-play announcers.

"KYLE moves down the ice, across the blue line and takes the pass from JUSTIN. KYLE passes to JASON and charges the goal. JASON shoots—blocked! KYLE is there for the rebound! KYLE shoots! KYLE SCORES! KYLE SCORES! KYLE SCORES!"

Kyle was actually still waiting for a face-off.

I was stunned. The match featured a dozen play-by-play announcers all narrating their own private games. Occasionally the color commentary paralleled the action on the ice, but usually the kids were rehearsing for The Action Yet to Come.

I was impressed, too. Any one of them could've made a Zamboni ride with an elderly pilot sound as exciting as game seven of the Stanley Cup finals. They cheered for their teammates, they diagramed their moves, they designed complicated plays on the telestrators in their unwashed little noggins—they played pretty well in person, but they were all Hall-of-Famers in the highlight reel rolling in their heads.

Until a different audience started showing up for hockey.

The following weekend we had games back in Indianapolis. The home rink for the Indy Junior Ice Squirt A team that year was the old Pan Am Plaza, a multi-level facility in downtown Indianapolis directly across the street from the RCA Dome, the original home of the Colts. Pan Am was newer and brighter than the Pepsi Coliseum, but it hadn't seen a fresh coat of paint since it opened in the '80s. The water fountains seldom worked, and every locker room had holes in the sheetrock. Pan Am had two rinks, one at ground level that was open and airy, and a subterranean pond that could chill the hardiest Canadian.

Pan Am was constantly in use, for public skating, figure skating, hockey, private lessons, birthday parties—the joint never seemed to close.

That Saturday morning, as my son and his teammates were busy practicing their "I just scored" stick-raising celebrations before a game with a team from Columbus, Ohio, a gaggle of preteen females wandered up to the boards. They had been figure skating in the lower rink and decided to take a look at the boys and one girl playing hockey in their home jerseys. The figure skaters gnawed on the preferred nutritional supplement of their species, watermelon-flavored chewing gum. You couldn't smell anything else.

The figure skaters twirled their hair around one index finger.

They twirled their gum around the other. They stood on one foot, then the other, heads tilted, batting their eyelashes at the rink in front of them.

Every boy—home and visitors alike—fell silent. The mood on the ice became as serious as a Senate hearing on gun control. Only the solitary girl with a hockey stick—little Amanda—kept a rap going: "The NHL's FIRST female winger sets and waits for the pass—AND HER BRILLIANT WRIST SHOT sails past the goalie's outstretched glove and AMANDA SCORES!"

The figure skaters cracked their gum and stared. The boys tried to avoid eye contact—with each other, with the girls, and especially with Mom and Dad. They were gonna be men now, dammit, and men didn't narrate their successes with a monologue that sounded like a bad imitation of Al Michaels calling the 1980 Olympic games.

They were men. Men who were utterly mortified by the idea that Mom and Dad were within one hundred miles of this very game. Mom and Dad *were* there, banging on the boards and telling the refs what for. Mom and Dad were getting their money's worth. Mom and Dad were shouting down those loudmouth thugs from the Buckeye State. Mom and Dad were embarrassing the hell out of Pookie and Num-Nums.

The shouts rained down on the boys from the parents in the stands: "KYLEJASONJUSTINTYLER! GET YOUR HEADU PTURNAROUNDCLEARTHEZONESKATE!"

The watermelon girls ignored the moms and dads stared at the boys. The dads stared at the girls, and the moms stared at everybody. The boys continued to look as if they were ignoring everything but the puck.

The watermelon girls began to comment on the game. Well, not the game so much, but the uniforms.

"Purple and silver and the black outlines—I have a blouse that has exactly those colors and it's soooo cool … Those little polar bears on the jerseys are soooo cute … See how the shirts lace up in front? That look is soooo retro, don't you think?"

The boys on the ice glanced at the girls behind the glass. The girls were talking to each other and pointing. The boys hunkered down, skated faster. They were determined. They were focused. They were certain that the girls were enraptured by their power, their speed, their control of the puck. They had no idea that the girls' interest in them was mostly aesthetic.

The parents kept yelling:

"KYLEJASONJUSTINTYLER! CENTERTHEPUCK! LOOKOUTINFRONT! CYCLEAROUND! BEHINDYOUBEHINDYOUBEHINDYOU!"

There was a tremendous crash as skater met skater by the boards near where the watermelon girls were watching the action and commenting on the colors. A kid from Indy and a kid from Ohio had met one another and the Plexiglas at exactly the same time. Both kids had come in low, eyeing the puck, and had tried unsuccessfully to pull away before impact. The kid from Columbus stiffened against the boards and then collapsed in a crumpled heap on the ice. The hit had pushed the facemask of his headgear into his nose violently, and the kid was bleeding profusely on the ice.

The moms gasped in horror. The dads gasped in empathy. The watermelon girls said, "EWWWWWWWW!" The kid from Columbus staggered to his feet and skated toward his bench, blood dribbling onto his jersey. His coach passed him off to his dad, who escorted the kid away from the rink. The parent and the child were sent to the concession stand for a plastic bag full of ice. As the kid and the parent walked by the watermelon girls, they all turned to look in silent awe. The kid wasn't crying. He was grinning from ear to ear.

The watermelon girls would remember him. His teammates

would speak of this day for many months. He had stained the ice red, and win or lose, he had shown those bums in Indy what a tough kid from Columbus was made of.

The kid knew that maybe one day, many years from now, this scene would be replayed in his adult life—except then maybe the ESPN cameras would be rolling.

"KYLE skates in low, and there's a TERRIBLE crash at the boards behind the net! There's an injury time-out as the trainer steps on the ice—but KYLE is up and skating toward the bench! I don't know how you define toughness in your town, but toughness has a name when it comes from Columbus—and that name is KYLE! KYLE! KYLE!"

Intermission: THE HOCKEY MOM

I've got to come clean at this point:

I've mentioned that hockey parents yell encouragement/criticism/idle threats from the stands. Not quite true.

Actually, it's the moms who do the bulk of the shouting.

I have noticed that, after watching thousands of minutes of youth hockey, it's the moms who generally seem to have more to say than the dads during the course of a game. There are more than one set of parents who had their roles defined thusly: Mom screams her head off, Dad shakes his head sagely.

Oh, sure, there are some dads who come uncorked so regularly you can set your watch by their manic episodes. Let's call one of these individuals "Yelling Man." Under the best circumstances, most of the other parents are able to move away from Yelling Man—he's content to scream by himself. The more distressing scenario is the one that features "Stalking Yelling Man." Stalking Yelling Man is the guy who rambles up and down by the side of the boards, following the play and jawing at everybody—his kid, your kid, the ref, the guy waiting to drive the Zamboni, everybody. Worst-case scenario: Stalking Yelling Man has the official title of *Coach* Stalking Yelling Man.

Despite what you know about youth sports, despite what you've heard about hockey, it's been my experience that the vast majority of dads at the rink are simply cheerleaders. A good play is rewarded with a vibrant "Attaboy!" while everything else is regarded with the wise stare of the inscrutable student of the game. It's Mom who's usually making all the noise.

My theory about this is simple: Moms don't care if they're wrong. If Pop is shouting, "Terrible call!" at a ref about some penalty that was obvious to the rest of the spectators ("Yeah, your kid *did* trip everybody but the goalie"), then Pop will feel terribly embarrassed. Pop should know better. Pop should have been paying attention. Doesn't Pop get it?

Mom can be wrong. Who cares? It sounds horribly sexist, but it's true. There is no pressure on Mom to make the right call. God forbid Mom should lean over to Dad and ask why Junior has been sent to the box, only to be met with a confused shrug. Dad missed the call. Dad doesn't know. Dad was looking at another hockey mom and thinking something less than wholesome. To admit a lack of knowledge is as bad for a dad as the admission that your nickname is Pookie is for a kid. It's embarrassing.

When my wife asks a question and I have no answer, I always have an excuse: "Sorry, dear, didn't see that play—I was taking notes."

The hockey moms from the Indy Junior Ice Squirt A Travel Hockey team were very keen on giving me their opinion when they found out that my incessant note-taking was for a book called *The Hockey Dad Chronicles*.

"Hockey *dad?*" went the refrain from every female parent. "Hockey *dad?* You're writing about hockey *dads?* Don't you think it's the *moms* you should be writing about? *We* dry the tears and wipe the bloody noses! *We* bring the snacks! *We* fill the water bottles! *We* make sure the little buggers have dry socks, for God's sake!"

Verily, ladies, I acquiesce. Yours is the greatest sacrifice. To give life, then watch it have its little ass kicked by some thug from Craptown, Illinois. Here is your tribute, a literary token of esteem, with apologies to the sacred poet:

The 23rd Mom

My Mom is the equipment manager, I shall not want
She driveth me to practice and very often games
She laceth my skates beside the frozen waters
She bringeth me Gatorade
She yelleth so that the other parents will not hear the coach
*   yelleth at me*
Yea, though I sit in the shadow of the penalty box
I will fear no ref, for Mom art with me
Thy spare stick and the time clock, they comfort me
Mom preparest a table of chicken nuggets between double-
*   header Saturday games*
She tapes up my stick, my puck flyeth quicker
Surely clean checks and slap shots shalt be mine all the days of
*   my life*
And I will dwell in the house of the rink every weekend

Hockey moms handle the organization of damn near everything. It's usually a hockey mom who's wearing an adult-size version of her kid's jersey (retail $79.99) with a photo button of her little tyke pinned to it (retail $9.99) and carrying a cowbell with the team logo on it (retail $12.99). Hockey moms organize the shipment and serving logistics of juice boxes, Gatorade, Rice Krispies Treats, and pizza bites between games. Hockey moms dress the kids' hotel room doors with crepe-paper streamers that match the team's colors when the Junior Ice are on the road. Hockey moms supervise the packing of clothing and the drying of gear.

Hockey moms construct the homemade noisemakers: the plastic water bottles filled halfway up with small beads in colors that match the team's jerseys. Hockey moms would shake these bottles filled with black, white, and purple plastic every time the Indianapolis Junior Ice Squirt A Travel Hockey team scored a goal. The rattling of all those beads in unison creates a noise that rings through the inside of the rink as loud as a jet engine landing on the center line.

Hockey moms make sure the skates are sharpened. Hockey moms pack the cooler full of pepperoni and apples for the road trips. Hockey moms sell scented Yankee Candles to raise funds for the team. Hockey moms will be the first to pipe up when an opposing team's parents start getting out of line. Hockey moms will pipe up just as loudly when their own husbands start getting out of line. Good luck telling an amped up hockey mom that *she's* out of line. That's her little Pookie or Num-Nums out there getting pummeled by those thugs from another state.

At some point in the season, word began to circulate that a few of the hockey dads had money riding on whether one of the hockey moms had been artificially enhanced. News of the bet came 'round to the subject of the wager. In true hockey mom style, the woman had casually mentioned the bet during a game.

"I hear you've made a bet regarding my breasts," she announced. The gutsier dads nodded and grinned; the rest of the bettors looked at their shoes.

"Well," she said, "I guess there's only way to settle it."

She crossed her arms and grabbed the bottom of her sweater. She'd begun to pull the thing off when the gambling dads stopped grinning and began to backpedal. "Uh, no, that's, that's alright, bet's off, we're fine, that's fine, thanks …" The other hockey moms gave the men in question looks full of daggers and venom as they grudgingly murmured approval for the brazen mom's behavior. A few of the hockey moms added, under their breaths, "Of *course* they're implants. Any idiot could tell."

Of all the hockey moms, my wife, Amy, suffered the most because of the nature of the game. Even an intentional plunging fall by one of the players resulted in a mortified gasp and a great gnashing of teeth from dear Amy. Whenever Oliver was on the ice, she held her hands palms inward on either side of her head like blinders, ready to cover her eyes in the case of a slash or a hit or a trip or virtually anything that befell our little skater. The poor woman was certain that the kid was destined to be carried off the ice on a stretcher every time he left the bench. At the beginning of every season, I was certain that This Would Be the Year. This Would Be the Year that I had to talk her into it. This Would Be the Year that I had to write the check myself. This Would Be the Year that I, and I alone, would be responsible for all of the driving and prepping and dressing of the child because Mom just couldn't bear to be involved any more.

The Year never came. That's because Amy discovered that ninety percent of all the moms felt exactly the same way she did—they just weren't nearly as demonstrative. In fact, at some point during the season when Oliver played for the Junior Ice Squirt A travel team, her hands dropped to frame her mouth. She started yelling.

Every time Oliver touched the puck, my wife yelled, "SHOOT!" Even if Oliver had possession next to his own goalie, the refrain went up: "SHOOT! SHOOT! SHOOT!"

I took one such opportunity to tug on her sleeve and say: "He can't. The goal he's shooting at is all the way down at the other end of the rink."

She bent in close to me. "I just don't know what else to yell," she confided.

"Okay," I replied, "you can yell 'shoot.' Just let me tell you *when.*"

The next time Oliver had a chance to fire one in, I gave her the cue.

"SHOOT!" she yelled.

Oliver shot. The goalkeeper smothered it. The ref blew his whistle.

"SHOOT IT AGAIN!" yelled Amy.

"The play's dead, lady!" said a hockey dad from the opposing team.

"Oh, whatever," whispered Amy.

I gave up. Amy yelled "SHOOT!" whenever she wanted to yell *something*. At least she was able to watch the kid play.

Amy had been asked, at the beginning of each season of our son's hockey career, to take on the mantle of "Team Mom." (This is akin to the rank of General in the hockey mom universe.) She had always declined, citing that her actual knowledge of the game amounted to little more than yelling, "SHOOT!" and being right about it roughly half the time.

This was probably a pretty good call on Amy's part. Even though she had the right kid experience as a preschool teacher, a fairly strong familiarity with the game was also a prerequisite for taking on the Team Mom title.

Team Moms are pretty easy to spot. They've usually decked

themselves out in spirit wear from head to foot—team logo fleeces and caps and jackets and sweaters, pants that match both home and away jerseys, buttons with the number or the picture of their little sniper beaming back at the viewer, clipboards and notebooks and schedules and data of every kind on every kid. The Team Mom, in addition to the aforementioned organizing of juice box purchasing assignments and the decoration of hotel room doors during away stands, is usually responsible for some form of record keeping. Whether she's next to the timekeeper counting shots and assists or behind the goal noting plus/minus stats (that's taking down the jersey numbers of which kids are on the ice when a point is scored for or against your team), the gig requires some puck smarts. Amy never felt comfortable with that aspect of the Team Mom job description.

Additionally, Amy always felt that the Team Moms were usually—well, over the top. Beyond all the yelling, Team Moms seemed to actually get upset when the team lost. Team Moms did a lot of the screaming when *their* young'uns screwed up. Team Moms bellowed and barked at the refs when the refs screwed up. And God forbid that the child of the Team Mom got less ice time during a match than the Team Mom felt was equitable—the coach could wind up pulling a scorekeeper's pencil out of his forehead after *that* post-game discussion.

Time-Out: THE HOCKEY PARTY

One of the critical things that the Team Mom is often responsible for is the organization of the Team Party. There are usually three parties: one at the beginning of the season so that every parent can get a gander at every other parent, one at Christmastime, and one at the end of the season so the kids can receive the trophies and plaques and trinkets that have cost you thousands of dollars in ice fees, gas money, pads, sticks, and trips to a heart specialist to treat you for stress and eating too many cheeseburgers on the road.

The first party is always billed as a getting-to-know-you mixer. This is often the moment when you realize that the Lunatic Screaming Brood that you've avoided for all these years has somehow managed to weasel its way into your little universe. You know it's going to be a long year when you notice that each and every Stalking Yelling Man and Over-the-Top Team Mom in the league is a part of your squad; yes, their progeny is now a winger or a goalie on your heretofore pleasant gaggle of kiddies and their elders. The initial party features questions for the coach and the Giving Over of The First Check. Alcohol is served to make the Giving Over of the First Check somewhat less painful.

When you meet the other parents, it's odd that there seems to be every type of parent represented on a particular team. I have heard that in some instances, a coach will take into consideration the behavior, demeanor, and even appearance of some of the parents when he's inviting kids to try out for his travel hockey squad. I know of one coach—who has divulged this information to me only with a promise of anonymity—who employs a codified system of noting what each and every parent is like next to the names of the kids on his short list of potential players. They break down as follows:

NG—Nice Guy or Gal; a parent who won't give you any grief.

PM or PD—Psycho Mom or Dad; a parent who simply must be put up with because their little Gretzky is the team's lead scorer.

GLM—Good Looking Mom. Do I need to explain?

More than once, a set of parents has shown up at an introductory party only to discover that the team is comprised almost entirely of under-achievers. A glance around the room reveals that the kids have all been given life by GLMs—and usually they've all been drafted by some coach who was recently divorced.

The Christmas gathering is almost always uncharitable. It's a time to bitch about the team's record if you're losing or your child's lack of playing time if the squad has a winning record. This is when you realize just how much you really cannot stand The Lunatic Screaming Brood since it consists of the folks who are doing most of the complaining. Alcohol is served to make listening to The Lunatic Screaming Brood somewhat less painful.

The final party in a season affords one the chance to see what parents have divorced one another in order to hook up with other parents on the same team. (The most controversial of these little games of rotating companions occurred at another team's party when, at the end of the evening, it became clear that two of the moms had become somehow romantically involved. The dads who attended this party claimed it was The Greatest Moment Ever in Youth Sports; those who didn't see it still dismiss it as an urban myth.) Alcohol is served to make looking at the record of a team mothered by GLMs seem somewhat less painful.

Trophies are handed out at the final party. One year that Ollie played, the mom considered by many to be the most GL of the GLMs was responsible for acquiring the prizes since she worked at a trophy-manufacturing place.

"Guess we really can call her a trophy wife," Amy said.

J

NOVEMBER—3rd PERIOD

Dayton, Ohio, seems to have more than its fair share of GLMs. I spent a good bit of the first game of Oliver's two-game stand in Dayton glancing around at the home team's moms. I must have been fairly obvious about it. Although she's generally not the jealous type, my wife, Amy, caught me and gave me an elbow in the ribs.

"Hey," I said defensively, "I should be allowed a little looky-looky after *that* drive."

We'd left Indy at 7 a.m. during a freak snowstorm that sent wave after wave of white powder blowing across I-70 eastbound. I'd been hunched over the steering wheel for two hours, white-knuckling the wheel while Amy read a book and Oliver snored in the back seat. Semi trucks blew past me and spattered ice and snow and salt and dreck across my windshield. I squinted into the distance as the wiper blades squealed and streaked across my vision. Three times in the first forty minutes of the trip I'd pulled over to refill the tank of blue stuff that jetted up from the hood and cleaned away the goo.

And all this, of course, after rousting a ten-year-old at 6 a.m. from his dreams of skateboards and bikes and Christmas just a month or so away.

My son, Oliver, is not what you'd call a morning person. I think perhaps most ten-year-old boys aren't morning people, granted, but this creature who we tried to wake a good ninety minutes before dawn was downright sub-human. He snarled and growled and bellowed and yapped and made the strangest guttural sounds as first his mother—and then I—tried to get the kid moving on a freezing Saturday morning. His mom started gently enough, stepping into his room and cooing, "It's time to get up now, honey."

Five minutes later my wife repeated the soft-sell approach.

Ten minutes later she tried bribery, shaking a box of Cinnamon Toast Crunch cereal just over his head.

Fifteen minutes later she dropped a rawhide bone on the kid's bed and sent our hyperactive Chesapeake Bay retriever into his room to fetch. The dog retreated twelve seconds later with her tail between her legs and no bone. Oliver had shoved the mutt right out his door.

Twenty minutes later my wife began turning on all the lights in the kid's bedroom and yelling: *"You're going to be late!"*

"Alright! Geez!" announced Oliver groggily—and then rolled over and pulled the covers above his head.

My wife came downstairs. "I've had it," she said to me. "Now you go get him up."

I threw open the kid's door and turned on every light in his room. "GET UP GET UP GET UP!" I hollered, banging the palm of my hand on the wall above the child's bed. Oliver hopped out of the sack.

I went downstairs. I smiled at the wife. "Nothin' to it!" I beamed.

His mom got angry.

Mom, you see, had to go through this five days a week. My job—radio show host on the morning drive program—required me to be at work at 4 a.m., long before it was time for Junior to rise and shine and get ready for another day of book-learnin' at school. As a result, my threatening bellow was something brand new to the child.

"You're going to come home every day at 6:30 a.m. just to wake him up," my wife said through her teeth.

After the kid had dragged himself downstairs to the breakfast table, then the monumental task of getting Oliver dressed, fed, and packed for a two-game stand in metropolitan Dayton became an actual hardship to me as well as the boy's dear mother. He didn't like this juice, he wanted that juice, he didn't like that cereal, he wanted that other cereal that we were almost out of, and he wanted potato bread toast and all we had was whole wheat.

He settled on an English muffin toasted cheese sandwich with that juice, not this juice. Done and done. Now we had to get the boy dressed.

During this particular time in Junior's development, he wanted to look exactly like the guys he idolized. Unfortunately, those guys were not all hockey players. Quite a few were the rappers he heard on the radio station where I worked at the time.

Time-Out: A FASHIONABLE MUSICAL INTERLUDE

My son has always been familiar with hip-hop artists—Lil Jon & the Eastside Boyz, 50 Cent, Snoop Dogg, Sean Combs, Puffy, Puff Daddy, P. Diddy, and Diddy (the last five being the same damn guy). My son, for a while, had memorized lyrics to songs that had been sung—sung? spoken? grunted? yelped? shpritzed?—by guys named Chingy and Nelly and Ludacris and so on. He asked for shirts that advertised bands with names that didn't seem to be much more than a combination of random letters and numbers, like D12 or Y2KFC (Okay, I made the second one up). He wanted to wear his hair short, very short and very bleached, and tried to lower his pants to levels where the pants weren't really pants anymore—they were a lot closer to the leg warmers some dancing female welder might have worn in a music video from the '80s. His mom yanked his pants up, so he turned his Yankees cap sideways.

For a while, I was raising Eminem. For a while, so was every hockey parent we knew. Some of the other folk railed against the notion that their ten-year-olds wanted to look like Phat Rhymin' Phools. Me and the missus were quite a bit more liberal than most.

Despite what you might first think when I tell you that a Marshall Mathers clone was living on my couch for a few years watching *SpongeBob SquarePants* on Nickelodeon and eating his body weight in Froot Loops every thirty-six hours, I wasn't terribly upset. I monitored the lyrics. I edited for content. I offered Parental Guidance even when it wasn't Suggested. I was Down With It.

So the kid was interested in hip-hop. So what? When I was a kid, my folks—especially my dad—made sure that my brother and I could pursue our interests in whatever cultural phenomena tickled our fancy. Back in the day, Pop was big into First Amendment rights, being an eager law student at the same time that I was approaching puberty. If I wanted to buy a George Carlin album and hear the hippie from Brooklyn recite the "Seven Words You Can't Say on Television," so be it. Carlin would rant,

Dad would explain. Richard Pryor would cuss, Dad would give it context. Dad was tolerant, and I vowed to be the same. Why the heck should I have a problem with the occasional off-color remark bellowing out of my kid's CD player? (Sure, we had to be careful with what was played in the hockey team's locker room—but home was a different story.)

Okay, okay, so Carlin railed against censorship and hypocrisy, and a lot of hip-hop tracks are about hookin' up wit bitches, doin' drugs, and gettin' money. Point against. The hip-hop lifestyle did give me pause—groupies and Bentleys and dope—until I thought about the stuff I listened to in junior high and high school and beyond. Which, as it turns out, was mostly about groupies and Bentleys and dope.

I'm pretty sure Plant, Page, Daltrey, Townsend, Jagger, and Richards weren't setting the text of *Little House on the Prairie* to power chords and honky-tonk blues riffs. Point for. Well, kind of. Rationalization for, anyway.

Think now—what is the difference between Ludacris—and if you don't know who Ludacris is, he's damn near the gangsta version of the next name I'm gonna drop—what is the difference between Ludacris and, say, David Lee Roth? None, of course, except for the fact that David Lee Roth is more palatable to Honkies of a Certain Age. He had guitars behind him, not a guy ruining a record and calling it rhythm.

So Eminem Junior liked hip-hop. So what? No worse than early Van Halen or anything by Ozzy, right? So my marvelous, academically talented, travel-hockey-playin' little Caucasian dug him some Phat Beats and Gangsta Ryhmes. Okay. I would advise, then consent, on occasion dissent, but I would remain proud in the knowledge that I retained an open mind, when, in fact ...

I was terrified by the trend.

Are you kidding me? Sagging pants and FUBU sweatshirts? Are you serious? Yankees caps in every color but Yankees blue and white, screwed down sideways and tilted atop a freakish dome of platinum hair? Ersatz ghetto lingo issuing from the jaws of my offspring as he flashed some ridiculous peace/victory/devil-horns/Crips/Bloods sign language with his pale little fingers?

Come on. Face it. The only white guy who can get away with dressing and sounding and acting and walking and talking like Eminem is—follow the logic here, folks—Eminem.

Memo to every other white kid in America who has ever attempted the aforementioned fashion statement: It ain't working. You look stupid, dawg.

And then ...

And then came Tony Hawk.

Thank you, Tony Hawk.

Thank you.

Tony Hawk rides a skateboard. He's my age. He rides a skateboard and does tricks and used to compete in the X Games on ESPN 2 until he retired to the land of virtual gaming. He rode a skateboard when I was a kid, back when I would do 360s and fakies and other tricks whose names I've forgotten on a wooden "Logan Earth Ski" deck that was as heavy—and as deadly—as the largest Louisville Slugger. Tony Hawk was riding in empty swimming pools on the California coast while I was turning my elbows and knees into hamburger on whatever funky asphalt I could find further inland.

At some point before I graduated from high school, I stopped riding a skateboard. Tony Hawk still rides his board for a living. Tony Hawk is a wealthy man. Tony Hawk is my age—and my boy thought he was the greatest.

My son saw Tony Hawk on television. Some kid he admired

at school dropped the name. So, my son wound up with a video game featuring Tony Hawk.

One fine winter Saturday morning, my son emerged from the basement where he'd been tooling through a Tony Hawk skateboarding adventure on his Playstation 2. He came up singing.

"I ... wanna rock and roll all night ... and party every day ..."

KISS? My son knew a KISS song?

"Where did you hear that?" I asked.

"'Tony Hawk's Underground.'"

See ya later, Snoop Dogg.

The fascination had begun. Pretty soon, riding the deck via a pair of thumb controls wasn't enough. The kid saved his pennies and bought a deck—with a healthy subsidy from Mom and Dad—that had all the proper accoutrements. The right wheels, the proper trucks (a "truck" is the whole axle and rubber bushing assembly under the deck), and the required airbrushed painting of some kind of hideous cartoon gremlin holding a bloody axe adorning the underside of the board.

As far as Oliver and most of the hockey team were concerned, second only to appearing in the Stanley Cup Finals was the dream of winning some strange plywood-riding competition in the X Games. Skatin' was hip, skatin' was cool, and somehow, some way, all his buds at school and on the team were picking up the fashion and the lingo and—thank you, Blessed Jesus—the music.

In the end, it wasn't KISS that was speaking to him. It was the stuff that was even louder—the stuff that went all the way up to eleven.

My boy grew his hair. He bought Converse Chuck Taylors— CONVERSE CHUCK TAYLORS! High-tops, no less!—and began trading in his hip-hop sweats for T-shirts that read: "Black

Flag," "The Ramones," and, believe it or not, "Pink Floyd." (I'm still trying to figure that last one out. The kid couldn't recognize a Pink Floyd cut even if Roger Waters was playing one live in our living room.)

This was all stuff I recognized. Stuff I recognized, God help me, from the '70s and '80s. Trucker-style baseball caps with the foam fronts and mesh backs. Shredded jeans. Wallets with chains on 'em. Black T-shirts with band names across the front. Long hair, down in the eyes. All the trappings of my youth, everything my old man had given me grief about—suddenly it was back. I would find my son thumbing through my record collection—the old vinyl stuff—looking between my old Waylon & Willie and jazz albums for needle-worn copies of the Dead Kennedys, the Sex Pistols, anything fast, angry, and most important, LOUD. (This was the same child who, a few short years earlier, had told me that "the big black CDs sounded too scratchy.")

I was giving my son and his buds a lift from our house to one of theirs when my son, thumbing through his CD case, produced a disc that I'd thought had somehow gone missing. It was one of the two CDs belonging to a small set I owned called *The Story of the Clash*. My son slid the disc into the player in my car and cued up "White Riot." He and his friends proceeded to sing along with the track—verbatim.

"White Riot"? Not only was the song written before the kid was born, but his dad hadn't even yet had a practice run at procreation.

Of course, more modern bands began to bleed from the speakers in his room—Green Day, Offspring, System of a Down—and I was geeked. All of this was, if not familiar, then at least palatable; I found myself becoming a born-again fan of the chunky guitar sound that is the very foundation of punk.

My wife harrumphed. "Y'know," said Mrs. W, "this was inevitable. This was all the crap he listened to in the womb."

Yeah, Nirvana rang through the house back in '91 and '92 whilst Junior was a-cookin'. Yeah, I always dug the loud stuff. But I sure as hell never expected my son's teenagerhood to sound so damned similar to my own. Dude.

Skatin'. Skatin' has brought back rock, dude.

Which leads me to the next conundrum.

How is this kid finally gonna rebel?

When will he get wise to the fact that his old man used to pull nose-grinds off the top of a ramp while somebody played "Teenage Lobotomy" out of a boombox? When will he realize that his dad *still likes* this stuff? What'll he do? Start listening to show tunes and standards? Wear a tie? Drink his milk? Clean his room? Am I creating the new millennium's version of Alex P. Keaton, the Reaganite character from the old TV show *Family Ties*?

Well, not yet.

As a result of his love for the skatin' life, the child's entire wardrobe now took a new and even more disturbing turn. Every item of clothing seemed to be covered with graffiti-style lettering underneath an embroidered flaming skull. The boy was draped from head to feet in baggy, dark cotton and denim emblazoned with weird gothic imagery and swirling slogans full of words that didn't seem to have enough vowels in them—he wore JNCO jeans. How do you pronounce JNCO? (Apparently, it rhymes with 'plinko'). My son looked like he was being recruited for a Mexican motorcycle gang.

Of course, when it came to fashion sense, there was one thing that both the skate culture and the hip-hop community had in common: an absolute disregard for that peculiar men's clothing accessory called "the belt."

As often as possible, Oliver tried to wear his pants as low as they could go. His mother screamed at him for letting his boxers show, letting his butt hang out, looking like a thug, a punk, or someone who was simply unable to dress himself. He'd wear long sweatshirts to cover up the fact that he was "sagging"— wearing his pants so low they might as well have been very large, expensive socks.

So, we compromised: Pull up your pants, or you won't play hockey.

It didn't stop the grumbling about it, but we always managed to get the kid dressed in a manner that made him look less like a candidate for jail time in L.A. and more like a Midwestern kid going to a hockey game.

RESUME PLAY

We had a two-game stint in Dayton and the weather was getting bad. I didn't have the time to argue about the height of the kid's beltline. We needed to simply get clothing on the boy's back and food into his belly.

After twenty minutes of cajoling to get the kid awake, fifteen minutes of arguing over a meal that took three minutes to eat, and another fifteen minutes of verbal sparring to get Oliver dressed with a belt, a shirt that was reasonably clean, a pullover (with the team logo on it, retail $29.95), a winter coat, and a stocking cap (spirit wear again, $9.99) we now had ten minutes to get the kid packed.

The gear went into the hockey bag—and we questioned the entire process.

"Do you have your helmet?"

"Uh-huh."

"Neck guard?"

"Yeah."

"Extra underwear?"

"I have everything I'm supposed to have, so quit buggin' me, okay?!?"

When we got to Dayton we discovered that Oliver had somehow forgotten his mouth guard. It was usually attached to the metal face-cage on the front of his helmet, but Ollie had removed the thing because "it got in my eyes' way when I was looking for the puck right at that spot."

"Oh crap!" Oliver announced in the locker room, using one of the Few Approved Swear Words for Ten-Year-Olds. "I forgot my mouth guard!"

Justin, a winger on the Ice, dug into his bag and announced brightly: "I got an extra!" Justin produced a piece of rubber resplendent with teeth marks and lint. He threw it to Oliver, and before his mother could raise a word of protest, Ollie jammed the thing into his grill.

"Hey!" said my boy through a mouthful of used tooth-protector, "ip fipps prebby goob!" (Translation: "Although the dental pattern of this protective device matches that of another child, it seems to conform adequately to my own unique upper masticators.")

His mom looked like she was going to throw up.

On the drive to Dayton that morning, though, Ollie's gear had been the last thing on my mind. Our compact wagon didn't seem to have enough traction to keep us on the interstate. I was just starting to consider pulling off the road and settling into a diner for a few hours when suddenly the storm abated and the road began to clear. I exhaled.

Amy looked up from the book she was reading. "Is everything okay?"

I was cranky; my back hurt from the tension of leaning forward into the wheel. "Yeah, yeah, fine, …" I muttered.

My wife knows my moods. She turned up the music streaming out the car's CD player and went back to her book. We usually love each other's company, but she could tell I was in no mood for chat.

At least Oliver was asleep. An only child awake for a long road trip could be torture on Mom and Dad.

Amy and I had taken to allowing Oliver to invite a pal along when we went on family vacations. His go-to pick was his teammate Taylor, whom everybody called "Taz" since he looked a lot like the Tazmanian Devil from the Warner Brothers cartoons when he skated—or did anything else, for that matter. Taz was a slight kid who wasn't afraid to scrap with guys who were twice his size.

The summer before Ollie joined Taz on the travel hockey team, Taz had a typical Taz-style run-in at a baseball game. Taz had been pitching during a Little League contest when the kid in the batter's box found out that Taylor was one-quarter Mexican, his grandmother being of Latin descent.

"Let's see what ya got, ya little wetback," said the thug with the bat.

Taz threw a fastball at the kid's knee—and connected. As the batter crumpled, Taylor charged off the mound and dropped his glove, freeing both hands to slug the bigot who'd offended him. The ump caught him as he cocked his right arm to clobber the batter, now prone in the dirt.

"Jesus, Taz," said the ump, "I was about to toss him for the 'wetback' thing."

Taz made the roadtrip bearable for long drives to northern Michigan or the Allegany Mountains or wherever our travels took us in the summer. During hockey season, Taz often spent the night before a big game so the guys could ride together. Taz had an older brother who also played hockey, and, sometimes, when his mom worked weekends or his dad picked up overtime, Taz's folks found themselves booked in three places with only two adults to cover the appointments.

Taz wasn't along for this ride. He'd gotten to the rink late and was suited up just in time for the pre-game drills. His tardiness was forgiven—the team was at least seven men down; parents had opted not to make the two-hour drive when they'd seen the radar picture of a sudden burst of frozen precip between Indy and the Ohio border. The team needed everybody they could get in a uniform. As it stood, the Junior Ice would have to play two games with a thin bench. The constant substitutions in hockey and the perpetual motions of players on the ice required at least several lines of three offensive players and at least a few pairs of defensemen. As it stood, we had two lines of offense and two lines of "D." By the start of the third period, the kids would be exhausted beyond all reason.

It was an odd pair of games—the kids knew that Dayton had a better squad, and they knew they'd have to skate like crazy to try and frustrate the overgrown snipers Ohio seems to breed. Taz spun constantly in front of the Dayton goal, slapping his stick against the ice and fidgeting while he looked for a pass. Oliver set himself up at the point—a corner of the ice just inside the blue line—ready for a puck that he could rocket toward the net and hope for a deflection or a rebound from Taz or anyone else that might give the Ice a goal and Ollie a nice mark in the assist column. It was working. The Indy kids were keeping the pressure on a team that looked to have more raw skating ability than they did. The Junior Ice hung tough for the first two periods of game one and entered the third period down a respectable 2-1.

Early in the third, a scrum erupted in front of the Junior Ice's goal. Oliver had tangled with a forward from Dayton who set up shop in front of the net, waiting for a teammate to feed him the puck, and Oliver had leaned on the kid. The pass from an Ohio winger found the blade of his partner in front of the Indy goal. The puck dribbled around just beyond the semi-circle in front of the net (called the crease) until the Ohioan swiped at it with the back of his blade. Matt the goalie fell forward and dropped on the puck, expecting a whistle to stop play now that he'd smothered it.

He hadn't. The puck trickled into the goal at a steady four miles per hour. Dayton 3, Indy 1.

In the years since Oliver first played travel hockey, we have discovered the unfortunate truth that the best goalies are the kids who are on a steady diet of Ritalin. Sure, it sounds as if ADHD and the art of net-minding might not be a winning combination, but the drugs that are handed out for ADHD seem to give a kid the unique focus and evening of mood that's required for a hockey goalie. The game unfolds slowly in front of the chemically zoned child, and the occasional errant puck that somehow manages to sail past the little lab monkey's glove, stick, or shinpad is nothing more than a temporary negative ripple in a very beautiful universe.

"Whoa. Bummer. Groovy shot, though, right, dude?"

Matt, the goalie, was not on kiddie Prozac. Matt the goalie felt the wheels coming off. He'd stopped twenty-six shots before the Dayton crew scored number three. It was a real crusher for Matt—the easy one you'd seen right in front of you and missed completely. Matt was down for the count; done for the day. The final score at the end of three periods: Dayton 5, Indy 1.

The second game ended with Dayton ahead 7–1.

After the kids sat in the locker room and listened to the coach make his perfunctory "Way to play hockey—we'll really take it to 'em when we've got a full boat" speech, after game pucks had been handed out for exceptional play to various kids (Ollie included, picking up a mention for four periods of tireless defense and two periods of dragging himself up and down the ice with the rest of his team), after we'd piled back into our car and found the interstate west back to Indy, my wife began her own speech.

"I really think that's the best you've ever …"

Her voice trailed off as she turned to look at the back seat. Ten minutes into our trip home, Oliver was sound asleep. We didn't need Taz for company on the ride back, either.

DECEMBER—1st PERIOD

Four days before Christmas, I volunteered to make the drive to Decatur, Illinois, by myself. No Hockey Mom for company. Hockey Mom wanted to stay home and get the house ready for the holiday, pick up a few last-minute gifts, etc.

Decatur was a three-hour ride from Indy, and the first game started at three o'clock in the afternoon Central Time. Indy was on Eastern Standard Time, and by the time the second game would wrap and we'd drive back, it was sure to be nearly midnight in Hoosierland. We decided not to sack in a hotel after the games—it was the holiday season, and our money was being spent on gifts.

We had left Indiana at about 11:30 a.m. Hockey Mom had packed us a cooler full of the usual stuff: apples, oranges, the ever-present Gatorade, a few sodas, and some salami and cheese. I threw my son's sticks and his equipment bag in the trunk and wheeled two-thirds of our family onto I-74 heading west. We shot past the little towns that dotted the Indiana prairie: Veedersburg, Mace, Waynestown, and Pittsboro, the home of NASCAR driver Jeff Gordon.

The plains rolled out ahead of us. We were driving through the long table of grassland and fertile fields that lies between the Appalachians and the Rockies. The land dips and undulates near Danville, Illinois, and then returns to a flat brown plateau toward Champaign/Urbana. We dipped southwest near the University of Illinois, home of the Fighting Illini, to make Decatur a full hour before game time.

Oliver was in the back seat of the car, his face pressed against the chilly window glass, watching the clouds overhead and glancing down at the shadow of our car as it raced over the asphalt below. Every yard of highway in this part of the Midwest was flanked by an identical tableau. Silos, corn, soybeans, cattle. The occasional truck stop, replete with a billboard advertising "XXX Adult Video SALE!" or "Lowest Tobacco Prices Allowed by LAW!" Food, gas, lodging—next exit. If you took every McDonald's in America and laid them end to end, well, you would've just built the U.S. Interstate System.

I slid a CD from its case and fed it into the slot in the dashboard. A voice from twenty years ago hollered, "ONE, TWO, THREE, FOUR!" and then a stampede of guitars thundered out of my little car.

My wife usually packed the CDs that we listened to on these road trips. She was convinced that no child should have a single second of educational downtime. The music she picked was almost always classical or seasonal, or something designed to improve the kid's cultural literacy. Stephen Foster, Gershwin, legendary Broadway musicals. Books on tape were another popular choice.

She'd also heard about something called "The Mozart Effect." Certain kinds of classical music seem to improve brain function when a person is exposed to that music just prior to performing a given task. My wife insisted that our son hear at least twenty minutes of Mozart before entering a rink. I'd brought the Mozart discs and forgotten about them entirely. The boy and I were listening to the Ramones.

Oliver was happy. After all, this was his music now, too.

It was four days before Christmas. My son and I were flying through the heart of the Midwestern United States in a Saturn sedan singing "Blitzkrieg Bop" at the top of our lungs. Happy Birthday, Jesus! Enjoy your day off, Hockey Mom!

I hoped my son would play well. Maybe I could convince Hockey Mom that there was some actual merit to my theory regarding the "Old School Punk Effect." Heck, it worked for Tony Hawk, right? It seemed to me that the Ramones were doing the trick. The boy was certainly geeked to play some puck.

We drove into Decatur. I held a sheet of directions in one hand and steered with the other. The town seemed to be not much more than a series of factories encircled by more factories with a rail line running through the middle of them all. A sign announced that Decatur was the soybean capital of the world. That was it. No famous comics or astronauts born here.

We passed the rink, deciding that we had enough time to stop at McDonald's and get something to drink. Coffee for me, a milkshake for the kid. Mozart and PowerBars? Not today! Hockey Dad is on the job, ready to pump junior full of East Coast punk and sugared dairy product!

We got our drinks and headed back toward the Decatur Civic Center. We passed a comic book shop with a sign in the window that proclaimed it was the "Home of Fatboy: Decatur's Largest Cat!" We didn't have time to verify Fatboy's existence or size, but I was amazed that nobody had called the Humane Society of Decatur regarding Fatboy's condition. Fatboy was clearly *not* consuming soybeans or anything else that resembled health food.

We parked in the lot that adjoined the Civic Center and wheeled our gear into the rink. The locker room hadn't been opened yet, so my son's teammates and their equipment bags were piled up in the lobby of the building. The Civic Center was the only semi-modern piece of architecture in town, a contemporary deep-red-brick '70s bunker that had been well cared for. The kids started playing hockey with balls of tape that had been pulled from the curved blades of their sticks.

"Cut it out!" shrieked a voice from near the door that led from lobby to rink. A snarling hag wagged a finger at the children. "Somebody might wind up in a hospital bed with that kind of crap!" she cautioned. She had all the charm of a Nazi dental assistant. Her job, apparently, was to make sure that anyone interested in public skating paid their admission. Her duties also included intimidating the visiting team. She stank of stale cigarette smoke and wore a faded Illini ball cap crookedly on her graying head. In fact, everything about her was gray—her skin had the ashen pallor of somebody who'd smoked for years. Her glasses were thick and cloudy, and she rasped at our kids in a gravelly voice. When the young'uns from Decatur began to trickle in, however, she smiled and cooed and patted them on the head. She was the picture of gentility.

Eventually, someone emerged from the depths of the Civic Center with a key to the visitors' locker room. Our players shuffled in and began to strip off the purple pullovers and black turtlenecks they were required to wear. My son opened his equipment bag, dove in to grab his undergarments, and promptly spilled the unconsumed half of his McDonald's milkshake into the hockey sack full of his pads.

All of it had to be scrubbed off. The shake had begun to coagulate and become sticky, so my work was critical. I must have sacrificed an entire old-growth forest with all the paper towels I used to try and clean off my son's hockey bag and the gear inside.

"Did Yzerman's old man ever have to do this?" I announced to the other parents in the room.

"No, but I bet his mom did!" came the reply.

About ten minutes before game time, all the parents were asked to leave the locker room. This happened before every game. The coaches outlined strategy or told dirty jokes or gave the kids the formula for cold fusion—we were never sure what went on during the pre-game chalk talks, and the kids were sworn to secrecy. My wife asked our son once: "What exactly do your coaches talk to you about when all the parents have to leave the locker room?"

My son gave her a look of utter determination. "Only the players and coaches of the Indy Junior Ice Squirt A Travel Hockey team are allowed to hear that information."

Hockey Mom was about to come uncorked. She had a look that said, "I'll tell *you* what I can hear after I carried you in my body and widened my hips giving birth and shelled out all this money and—" but I intervened before she could get started.

"I'm sure it's fine. My Pop Warner football coach used to do the same thing."

"And what were those little talks about?" demanded Hockey Mom.

"He told us how to pick up chicks," I said.

Hockey Mom glared and punched me in the arm.

I wandered down the hall and stood with the other parents by the doorway in the boards that led directly to the ice. The team trundled out a few minutes later, chalk talk over, their skates thumping on the rubberized floor. Every skater knew the rule:

Nobody out on the ice until the big doors had closed behind the Zamboni. Every door to the boards had to be shut before a skater took the ice. The purpose here was simple—nobody ever need be run over by a Zamboni. (Additionally, with all the doors shut, an errant puck couldn't come screaming off the rink and smack an inattentive hockey parent someplace soft and/or deadly.) At the moment the boards clanged shut at the other end of the rink, it was time to take a lap and start the warmups. The kids slapped their sticks on the ice in unison, then ran three minutes of shooting drills. They assembled at the net, raised their sticks in the air, and chanted "Let's go ICE!"

A buzzer sounded. Indy and Decatur lined up. The goalies each held a glove up, a signal they were ready. The striped shirt dropped the puck.

The clock began to run as Jared won the face-off. Jared was Indy's lead scorer. Jared's dad was the team manager and part-time coach. Jared's mom came to each and every game. Jared was an assistant captain and probably the team's best stick-handler. Jared and the rest of the team looked downright evil in their away jerseys: dark purple and black with black helmets, pants, and gloves. Jared scored easily in the first twelve seconds.

The kids skated effortlessly. They changed shifts on the fly without getting hung up. No one burned our defense, but our shooters certainly burned theirs.

It was a long day for the team from Decatur. It was a pair of easy victories for the Indy Junior Ice. It was a great day for Hockey Dads and Ramones fans everywhere.

It took two weeks to get the smell of sour milk out of my kid's hockey bag.

Intermission: GEAR

The hockey bag itself is larger than the average coffee table. Oliver's gear carrier was a monstrous piece of silver and black luggage that ran to a length of five feet. Nearly two feet high and two feet wide, the bag had a retractable handle on one end and a set of wheels on the other. The wheels—the same kind you'd find on a pair of in-line skates—were set very wide on the bottom of the bag. The bag's best feature was a complicated set of zippered panels that opened up to another layer of panels underneath that were made out of mesh netting. The netting held the gear in the bag while allowing the equipment inside to air out and lose a little of the horrific stench that emanated from all hockey gear.

The stink of the hockey player's armor is the stuff of legend. The junior aroma was no different. They were soaked with sweat on the inside and drenched on the outside by numerous falls to the surface of the rink. The ice under the skater's feet was always polluted with a potpourri of metal shavings, spit, and Zamboni exhaust. The end result, to my nose, was akin to what a wet dog would smell like if you hit him with a load of pepper spray. *Eau de maced canine du aqua.* As soon as the family made it home from a hockey game, the first order of business was decontamination.

The post-game ritual ran this way: When Oliver got home, he emptied the bag. Immediately. The gear was hung out to dry on an ancient metal coat tree in the garage. The soaking underclothes, socks, and jerseys went right into the washer. Liberal doses of Lysol were applied to the door closest to the equipment. Candles were lit. Prayers were said. The EPA was petitioned—only federal funding could buy the stuff necessary to sanitize Oliver's pads.

God forbid the temperature dropped below freezing in the garage. Then Ollie's pads would be pulled into our laundry room to keep them from freezing up. Nothing's more awful than pulling frozen hockey pads over an exposed thigh, and we lived with the stench until I broke down and finally added a heater to our insulated auto hangar.

It hadn't always been this way. The kid hadn't always been this stinky. As a six-year-old, he'd needed help putting on the pads, too, each and every one. You'd start by outfitting the kid in either long johns or pajamas. Usually the pajamas contained images that ran in direct contrast to the nature of the sport. The goalie on Oliver's Mite All-Star team was a little girl named Amelia. After one game, Amelia's folks were pulling off her pads to reveal her flannel sleepwear, which was covered with identical pictures of dolls. My wife called out, "Great game, Amelia!" Amelia looked at Amy, smiled, then pointed to one of the pictures on her pants leg. "I'm getting *this* Barbie for Christmas!" she announced.

Over the pajamas went the cup. No explanation was needed here, especially for the boys. Either the cup came attached to a pair of boxers that included Velcro tabs for the leggings, or you could opt for a garter belt to hold up the hockey socks. (Really. No kidding. A garter belt. Not real manly, huh?)

After he'd wrangled himself into the cup, the shinpads went on. If you've ever seen a child's shanks after a pick-up street hockey match, you'll know how critical shinpads can be. The hockey socks—which absolutely always matched the jersey—went on over the shin protectors and clipped to either the Velcro or the belt. Some parents also wound clear tape around the socks to tighten them up.

Next, the hockey pants. Hockey pants are padded throughout.

Fall on your butt, the tailbone's covered. Puck to the thigh, there's a pad there. The pants ride high on the player, covering the kidneys in the back.

After the pants, there's the shoulder and chest combination. This bit of business makes your baby boy look like a *Star Wars* stormtrooper. The chest plate drops low across the solar plexus, and there's a plate in back of equal length. The elbow and forearm pads are installed, the top of the elbow pad touching the very bottom of the shoulder pad. Next, you assist the child as he attempts to wriggle into his jersey, his yelps of pain causing you to realize you've been trying to force the poor little bugger's skull through the sleeve.

The neck guard is wrapped around his gullet and sealed shut with Velcro tabs. The helmet with a full-face cage is strapped on. A mouth guard, dangling from the cage, goes into the kid's chops. You'll worry more about the mouth guard later in the child's life, when his baby teeth are replaced by payments for his orthodontist's Jaguar.

The kid always puts on the gloves himself, no matter how old he or she is. Your child is now ready to play hockey. He is completely covered in plastic, foam rubber, vinyl, and Velcro body armor. The only part of your child exposed to the action is a small strip of unprotected flesh in the middle of his calf. This tiny area is where your child will be hammered by an errant puck within the first ten seconds of the first period of the first game of the season.

This is the only thing that can really damage a hockey player at the age of five or six. A child who collapses on the ice is usually feigning injury, fully aware that he is in the ultimate position of control. (DRAMA at its finest, youth hockey style.) He has a) stopped the game completely on his account alone, b) garnered the attention and/or pity of every adult in the rink, and c) guaranteed himself several helpings of ice cream and/or pizza that will be purchased after the final buzzer by his sympathetic mom.

You have to love a kid who is willing to put up with all this for a lousy game. That is the thing about most hockey players that continually amazes me: These kids get up at five o'clock on a Sunday morning to pull on thirty pounds of frozen pads and run headlong into a hard plastic wall. Sure, they all have that same charming disposition when they struggle out of their warm beds, but when it sinks in that they've woken up to play some puck, dang, now that's a good reason to get goin'! What the hell motivates these children? Why does a kid who acts like cleaning up his room is akin to a life sentence at slave labor willingly volunteer to suffer through the preparation that hockey requires?

As for Oliver's Junior Ice Squirt A team—children at Squirt level can pretty much dress themselves. The kids really only need help with lacing up the skates. The kids like them tight—it's amazing how tight. So tight a foot-bound Chinese empress would complain. This is the one moment where Hockey Mom will often yield to Hockey Dad. "He doesn't like the way I do it, so why don't *you* lace his skates so he stops complaining!"

"Gladly!" responds Superhero Hockey Dad. "Only my Superhero Hockey Dad strength is a match for these laces!"

Halfway through the first period, your child will then demand that Hockey Mom come down to the bench. "Mom, can you loosen my skates? My left foot's asleep or something."

Of course, after having shelled out for all this state-of-the-art protective wear, at some point you'll learn that junior really doesn't need a nickel's worth of gear to engage himself in hockey. A vivid example of this was given me while I was killing time in the lobby of Perry Park, a rink in southern Indy, while I waited to see Ollie take the ice against the visiting Decatur Flames.

The parents of the Flames were sitting around in the lobby, and they were a bit grumpy because our team had pretty much taken it to their little fellas the last time we'd tangled. I could hear bits and pieces of the conversations the Decatur folk were having. The visiting parents were engaging in the time-honored tradition of assessing blame elsewhere for their children's poor performance against the Junior Ice.

The refs had been lousy. The Ice players were dirty cheaters, cheap-shot artists, sneaky little devils who'd throw an elbow or a knee when the ref was skating away from the play. And as for the Flames? The coaching was poor, their best shooter was sick, their goalie was distracted because his dad had left his mom for that woman from Chicago, and so on.

(Sometimes, folks, your child's team will be better than the other child's team. And sometimes, folks, your guys will simply be worse.)

A kid sitting next to me on the bench where I'd perched was watching Nickelodeon on the lone TV in the lobby. He'd obviously just played a game himself—he was wearing hockey pants, skates, a down coat over a soaking-wet T-shirt, and a stocking cap that looked to be about three sizes too big. It towered above his head like a big black finger, flapping back and forth as he moved his noggin. The kid was methodically consuming a flavored ice drink by scooping the contents out of the cup with one of those combination straw/spoon things. He'd scoop, raise, slurp; scoop, raise, slurp. The pacing was completely even. Scoop, raise, slurp. Scoop, raise, slurp. The sound could've served as a backbeat for a hip-hop act. Scoop, raise, slurp. I imagined a bass line matching the rhythm of the kid's work. Scoop, raise, slurp.

Suddenly the kid stopped. He looked at the bottom of his cup. Empty.

The child then exhibited one of the natural instincts of the youth hockey player. For a youth hockey player, the secondary purpose any kind of disposable item whose primary function has been completed, depleted, or exhausted is best expressed as:

Puck.

Ball of stick tape that you've just peeled off the blade? Now it's a puck. Empty plastic Powerade bottle? Puck. Discarded hubcap? Puck. Old shoe? Puck. Dead squirrel? Well, I've heard a story in the locker room about *that* disgusting scenario, but decorum prevents me from repeating it.

The kid stood, crumpled up the cup, dropped it on the floor, picked up his stick (which was leaning against the wall under the sign that read "NO HOCKEY IN THE LOBBY") and tried to smack the cup into a trashcan across the room.

A crumpled paper cup with a wax coating has aerodynamic properties that are decidedly different than those of a hard rubber disc three inches in diameter and one inch thick. Said cup also has another major difference from said puck: It is impossible to empty a Slurpee cup of all its contents—unless, of course, you launch it across a room with a hockey stick.

The kid wound up and gave the cup a terrific slap shot. The cup arced across the room, spinning delicately in the air as it sprayed a fine mist of cherry-red Slurpee goo over the heads of several hockey moms and dads from Decatur. The kid had missed the trashcan wide left by at least seven feet, but had somehow managed to drop the cup directly into someone's serving of cheesy nachos at the snack bar. When the owner of the nachos bellowed "HEY!" in a booming, angry baritone, the kid snapped to attention as if he'd been awakened from a dream. The child had simply been performing involuntary motor functions up to that point. He didn't know where he was; he didn't care, and it didn't matter: Garbage equals puck, stick must meet puck. There are no variations.

Unfortunately for the kid, his old man had witnessed the whole event. Nowhere to run. Nowhere to hide. Justice was meted out swiftly. Pop hauled junior out of the lobby by the collar of his coat, snarling at the kid through his teeth. "How many goddamn times do I hafta tell ya about this sorta thing …" The kid was wide-eyed with fear. What would the sentence be? The stocks? The gallows? No Nicktoons for a month?

Nacho man chuckled. A Decatur parent harumphed. She murmured, just loud enough for a good portion of the lobby to hear, "These Indy children. You would never see our little men on the Flames do such a thing."

That afternoon, the Decatur Flames set a record for penalty minutes at Perry Park.

Time-Out: THE BOX

Speaking of penalties…

Every hockey mom and dad has been asked—and many have declined—to serve time as a scorekeeper, timekeeper, or penalty box attendant. Of these, the least stressful is the role of penalty box attendant. The gig is simple: Wait in the box with the offending party, yell when the penalty's almost up, then crank open the big door and shoo the little criminal out of the doghouse when the penalty clock reads double-zero.

Naturally, penalty box attendants man their own team's box. This affords the occasional rare opportunity for you to jaw at your own kid in direct, one-on-one fashion during the course of a game. There are three types of parents in this situation:

1. The Critic

This parent is simply upset. Upset with his kid for doing something dumb or, more often than not, upset with the ref for seeing junior do something dumb. This parent will yell, scream, cajole, carry on, and generally make it clear that the wrong individual has been pressed into service as penalty box attendant.

2. The Psycho

This is the parent who firmly believes that junior was properly called for interference, tripping, high-sticking, or whatever—and simply doesn't care. This parent can't wait to chat with her little cement head about either how to get away with it next time or, worse, to go ahead and exact revenge on the little wimp who drew the foul last time. This parent will yell, scream, cajole, carry on, and generally make it clear that the wrong individual has been pressed into service as penalty box attendant.

3. The Harrison Ford (or Gary Cooper, depending on your age)

This is the quiet one. This individual is often such a student of the game that he realizes that either a) although the call was bad, these things tend to even out by the end of the game, or b) his darling little thug actually screwed up. The other kind of silent types are folks like me—people who are still learning the game and don't want to look like a schmuck for saying anything that might sound even a little off-base. Harrison Fords are the types who are often asked to man the penalty box on numerous occasions. If you are being pressed into service during the course of the game, this is the job to have. Rarely will anyone heckle you for the simple act of opening a door.

Keeping time is another matter entirely.

Timekeeping is the most stressful activity for a hockey parent to undertake—besides, of course, the role of coach. The home team usually supplies parents to man the buzzers and digits. If you get picked, God be with you. You've got to start and stop the clock at just the right moments. Puck gets dropped, you better start the clock. Whistle blows, you better stop it.

Suppose your team is up by a goal with fifty seconds left. The other team takes a shot at your net and the puck gets hung up someplace on the back of the net. The ref blows the whistle. Let the clock run a millisecond long and the team that's down a goal will scream at you for trying to run time off the clock for the home squad while they're ahead. If you see the stoppage in play, and say, throw the timepiece into park a moment *before* the ref whistles it dead, your own allies will turn on you like a pack of rabid dogs in a chicken coop. Me, I don't need the stress.

I once volunteered to run the clock during one of Oliver's hockey games when he first started playing the organized version of the sport (with goalies and everything, no orange cones). I quickly realized that if I erred by even a fraction of a second, too early or too late, this apparently gave certain parents the inalienable right to refer to me as someone who had relations with either certain barnyard animals or my own mother. And Mom, according to those folks, is also apparently double-jointed.

I have been pressed into service more than once to serve as the official scorekeeper for a game. Usually, this is pretty easy. You're given a large form to scribble on, and it's your job to tally shots on goal (and, of course, saves), points scored, assists, and penalty minutes logged. Since the ref will skate over to the scorer's table and give you detailed info about who scored, who assisted, and who committed what infraction to earn a trip to sit with Harrison Ford, all you really have to pay attention to is the number of shots either team fires at the net.

Easy, right?

The last time I kept score—I repeat, the *last* time—a hockey mom from the opposing team decided to perch on my shoulder to check the count. It was clear from her dress and demeanor that she was an over-the-top team mom. It was also clear from her screeching critique of the net-minder that she was the goalie's mom. The woman held a clicker—an automatic counter like one you'd use if you were a bouncer at a nightclub making sure that the place wouldn't violate the fire department's "maximum persons" edict—and kept her own tally of shots. At the end of every period, she checked my work.

After period two, she told me I'd shorted her squad two shots.

"I don't think so," I said.

"YOU NEED TO BE MORE ACCURATE," she bellowed. "THIS IS A LEAGUE GAME."

"Oh, I'm sorry—does your ten-year-old get a cash bonus if he stops more than twenty?"

The guy keeping time was laughing so hard he started the clock ten seconds late into the third period.

Every game that I've attended, I've been asked to do the simple stuff. Man the penalty box. Keep score. Now, I always decline. I learned long before Ollie's Squirt season to act dumb. I didn't want to get into a shouting match during a hockey game played by ten-year-olds. During Ollie's Squirt season, my wife and I volunteered to a) bring food, and b) make sure the water bottles were filled. Sure, somebody could claim you brought the wrong kind of cream cheese for the bagels, but that wasn't a game-breaking situation, now, was it?

J

DECEMBER—2ⁿᵈ PERIOD

Oliver has always been a tall kid. His size helped his position on defense on the hockey team. At the age of ten, his hair was dirty blonde, darker in the winter, but he and his teammates had insisted on getting the tops of their heads frosted with lighter colors. All but two kids had the look, which made for a weird uniformity among the Junior Ice Squirt A Travel Hockey team even when their helmets were off.

The hockey moms who'd lightened their children's hair spent their time in the locker room talking about how cute their boys looked—and how some had complained bitterly about the smell, the application, the whole process of getting a head full of highlights. Cody's mom went over to her son and tousled his hair. She was a professional makeup artist who owned her own cosmetology shop. "He hated the whole business of it, but it was worth it. He's so adorable with this frosting, don't you think?"

The boys on the Indy Junior Ice Squirt A Travel Hockey team wore the exact same expression as their dads. Adorable was *not* the look they'd been going for.

Oliver, though, with his height and his bulk and the frosted noggin, did not look adorable. He was starting to look downright mature. The baby fat was leaving his face and his jowls were narrowing into a jaw line that framed an ever-more-prominent chin. He still played with toy cars and built fantastic machines with his LEGO blocks, but more and more I'd find him talking on the phone or listening to CDs through a set of headphones. MTV was slowly beginning to replace Nickelodeon.

The year that he played travel hockey with the Junior Ice Squirt A squad was the first year in memory that he didn't write a letter to Santa Claus.

On the eve of my son's tenth Christmas, right around dinnertime, it began to snow. My family and I went to visit some friends, then slid through the streets of Indianapolis to church.

The service included a call-and-response portion. Words and directions had been printed in the bulletin. The pastor spoke a line, then the left side of the congregation responded, then the right. My son, who'd only experienced anything remotely like this at sporting events, naturally assumed that the object of this exercise was to find out which half of the crowd could be louder. He read from the bulletin at the top of his lungs. Other families stared. I decided I'd better either take the kid to church a lot more or not at all.

Oliver had a white Christmas that year. By the morning of the twenty-fifth, seven inches of heavy, wet snow lay on the ground, with more on the way. Oliver's gifts were, for the most part, hockey-related: a small version of arcade bubble hockey, a new equipment bag, a knee hockey goal of his own. Oliver now owned every home-hockey game known to man, from the simple box with sticks called Nok-Hockey, to a full-size air hockey table complete with automatic scorer, to an NHL video game for Playstation 2. The kid was obsessed, and his mom and dad indulged the madness.

Of course, Oliver is an only child, and only children are indulged. Only children do not have a brother or a sister tagging along to the rink, trying to amuse themselves any way they can. Often we'd see the little sisters of some of the players playing with Barbie dolls as they crouched just outside the ice, never flinching when one of their brothers or one of his teammates hammered into the boards with a resounding, booming crash that made every adult in the venue wince. One can only imagine what went on inside the brain between those pigtails: "Maybe if something *really* bad happens to Kyle, then I can have his room."

A sibling comes in handy, however, for entertainment during those long stretches between games. The kids trade their skates for tennis shoes and pull off all their hockey gear save for the pants and shin pads. Add a bottle of Gatorade and a fresh T-shirt, and you're ready for a spirited round of "Making Kyle's Little Brother Run and Hide."

Feeding Kyle's little brother was pretty amusing as well. The boys had convinced Kyle's little brother to lie flat on his stomach at the bottom of a wheelchair ramp between games at Pepsi Coliseum on a Saturday. The child had his mouth open and half of the Junior Ice team was trying to roll Skittles candies into the kid's gullet from the top of the incline. Things were progressing without incident until it was Kyle's turn to try and roll a Skittle into his kid brother's face. He missed.

"Ha, ha," said the tyke, "you suck!"

Kyle threw a Skittle at his brother's head.

"Ha, ha," said the tyke, "you throw like a girl!"

Kyle then decided to alter the experiment. Kyle decided to see if his brother would be able to swallow a hockey puck that was thrown at him like a fastball. Fortunately for kid brother, kid brother knew how to duck. Unfortunately for Kyle, kid brother told Mom about the incident, and Kyle was off the hockey roster for a full two weeks.

Oliver never got grounded for beating on his siblings. Oliver did get grounded, however, whenever anything had been broken and the item in question had surely been destroyed by someone under the age of twenty-one; Ollie didn't have anyone else to blame things on.

Still, Oliver got to do what he wanted pretty much when he wanted—there wasn't another kid with a vote, a brother or sister who wanted pizza instead of a burger or a trip to the video arcade instead of mini-golf. Oliver wanted to go sledding on Christmas Day, so sledding we went.

After all the wrapping had been thrown away and the breakfast dishes cleaned up, we drove to the parking lot at the bottom of Butler Hill. Before the arrival of an apartment complex that wiped out one of Indy's few slopes, Butler Hill lay at the foot of Butler University, between the old football stadium and 52nd Street in Indianapolis. (It was in full view of Hinkle Fieldhouse, where the final scenes of the film *Hoosiers* were shot.) The hill sloped down from the college toward the old canal and into the flood plain of the White River. This part of Indy is where many of our Non-Hockey Friends live. (This is one of the early warning signs that you've become a Hockey Mom or a Hockey Dad. You separate your adult acquaintances into "Hockey Friends" and "Non-Hockey Friends." You will be invited to Non-Hockey events by and with your Hockey Friends, but someone will inevitably wind up talking about hockey.) A few of our Non-Hockey Friends had trudged up from their riverside neighborhood called Rocky Ripple to enjoy the afternoon with us.

The top of Butler Hill backed to a stadium wall that was covered with psychedelic graffiti. A small ledge separated rider from slope. Since it was one of the few hills in Indy, and since it was pretty wide as well, the damn thing was truly dangerous. It got icy quickly from all the use it saw, and there was no single path back to the top. Climbers staggered away from sledders who seemed to have zero control over their machines; no matter whether you were coming up or flying down, it always seemed as if most of the crowd was headed in the other direction, and they were all about to run into *you*.

Because Butler Hill University lay at the border of two neighborhoods, one decidedly wealthy and the other decidedly not, you could get a look at every imaginable type of sled-like vehicle ever conjured. From toboggans that looked like they'd been ordered the previous day and shipped via rush delivery directly from L.L.Bean in Freeport, Maine, to oddly cut chunks of half-inch-thick particle board, everybody dragged their rides to Butler Hill to democratically bang the shins of everyone who was too dumb to look up as he struggled to the top of the hill.

Our friends Dan, John, and John's daughter Helen had made the trip up to the hill from Rocky Ripple. Both Dan and John had long hair—in fact, Dan was regularly mistaken for Howard Stern; he looked just like the guy. John took several sedate toboggan rides with the kids while Dan opted to rocket down the hill by himself. Dan took a running start and went sailing down the slope headfirst every time. At the beginning of every run that Dan made, Ollie and I had taken to yelling, "Watch out! Projectile hippie!"

The bottom of Butler Hill flattened suddenly as it met a small service road that was plowed only on workdays. When it was bare, the asphalt ground the bejesus out of anything you were riding. A sled with metal rails made a really horrible sound. Even with a base of crystal, the abrupt change in angle wrenched the backs and hammered the knees of aging brats like the hippies and me. The kids didn't notice a thing. Dan and John expressed relief that they wouldn't have to work for the rest of the week—they had time to recover from acting like a ten-year-old.

I wasn't so lucky. In forty-eight hours, I had to fold my bruised lumbar vertebrae into a compact car and drive Junior to a series of games in a faraway city. The Junior Ice had been invited to a tournament two states south. In addition to every other expense, travel hockey was now buying my chiropractor a nicer boat.

Christmas was on a Wednesday. My wife pulled down all the decorations on Thursday. On Friday, we drove to Nashville, Tennessee, for the Southern Ice Lightning Hockey Invitational. The Southern Ice Lightning Hockey Invitational would be held, officially, in Franklin, Tennessee, and would include teams from Mite, Squirt, and Pee Wee divisions. "Southern Ice" was the name of the arena. "Lightning" was the name of the team.

The invitational drew teams from some pretty far-flung locations: The Baton Rouge Kingfish were there, along with the Kenasaw Lazers, the Memphis Blues, and the Evansville Thunder.

I've always wondered who comes up with the names of these teams. The Baton Rouge Kingfish? Who else plays in Louisiana? The Skatin' Cajuns? The New Orleans Andouille Sausages? The Shreveport Rednecks?

Time-Out: TEAM NAMES

The Nashville Lightning was a pretty interesting name, one of those team monikers that originates from local weather patterns or natural disasters peculiar to the area. There's a professional soccer squad in California called the San Jose Earthquakes, and there must be more than a hundred various collegiate and professional sports in tornado alley that call themselves the Cyclones. Why in God's name would anyone want to name a sports team after the absolute worst aspect of their hometown?

How about the Compton Drive-Bys or the Detroit Unemployed Drunks? The Bronx Gang-Bangers or the Staten Island Cosa Nostra Stoolies? Three cheers for our New Jersey Toxins! Let's hear it for our Las Vegas STDs! And a warm welcome for the visiting team, Seattle's Anal-Retentive Double-Income No-Kids Yuppies Who Moved Here from L.A.!

DECEMBER—3ʳᵈ PERIOD

We left for Nashville before dawn. The snow on the ground began to diminish as we headed into the middle of the Hoosier Uplands and on through the hills of Kentucky. We passed Abe Lincoln's birthplace and drove south toward the heart of the old Confederate states. Amy kept cautioning me about my speed. Even though our car had Indiana plates, she was sure that a Southern cop's radar could pick up on the fact that she hailed from Buffalo, New York. She was certain that her Yankee heritage was a crime in and of itself in any state that had fought for secession in the nineteenth century.

There was no hiding the fact that Amy was a Northern girl. She spoke with a deep Great Lakes accent—and, just like anyone else from Lake country, when she got excited, she honked like a Canadian goose.

I deferred and slowed as we drove through Kentucky. An endless array of brown highway signs announced various tourist attractions: Diamond Cave, Mammoth Cave, Maker's Mark Distillery. Kentucky is big on spelunking and tours of bourbon plants. I don't recommend mixing the two.

South of Bowling Green, Kentucky, we decided we were hungry. Nothing in the cooler we'd brought looked appealing, so we succumbed to temptation and ate at the dreaded drive-thru.

I challenge anyone in America to stop at a fast-food restaurant within one mile of an interstate highway and try and order something that doesn't have cheese on it. The Breakfast Croissanamuffin, the McWhopper, the Extra-Value Biggie Cardiac Classic—the names are different, the sauces might change, but the basic ingredients are all the same: slab of meat on starch with cheese.

The road stretched out ahead of us as we ate. Amy played Mozart for Oliver. I vowed to eat nothing but salad for three days after this road trip.

We rolled on into Tennessee. Eastern Time gave way to Central, and we gained an hour as we headed down I-65. This meant we'd have time to check in at the hotel and relax a little before the first face-off at 4 p.m. local time. The next day was full, too: two youth games in the morning and an NHL game at night. The organizers of the tournament had reserved a section of nosebleed seats of the Gaylord Arena in Nashville for the families participating in the tournament. The Gaylord was the home ice of the Nashville Predators NHL team, which was playing host to the defending Stanley Cup Champions that year, the Detroit Red Wings. Oliver had brought his Red Wings jersey to wear at the game.

There was some discussion as to whether or not this would be sportsmanlike. My wife insisted that since the folks from Nashville were kind enough to invite us to the tournament, then it was our duty to don the blue and bronze of the Predators during the game. I reminded my wife that our attendance at the tournament included dumping about seven hundred bucks of our hard-earned money into the Nashville economy, and I felt the kid should wear whatever the hell he wanted to. Besides, I told her, Detroit was the reigning champion of the league. A lot of bandwagon riders would be wearing red.

My wife disagreed. Her reasoning wasn't all about sportsmanship: She was a proud Yankee, but she didn't want anybody in Nashville to know it.

I wondered about the NHL game myself. Hockey in Nashville? How many people would actually be there? How many of the locals had even the slightest understanding of a cold weather sport that didn't involve a pigskin? Was somebody going to play the Canadian national anthem on a banjo?

We checked into the hotel and got settled. Oliver wanted to go swimming with some of his teammates who'd already arrived. The hotel was fantastic: Every family had a two-room suite with a fridge and a microwave, and all the rooms faced a balcony that encircled an open atrium nine stories high. Even though we were getting a terrific deal on the accommodations, this joint was a good bit pricier than the places we usually stayed.

We drove to the rink an hour before game time. The weather was warm and sunny, no snow in Dixie this Christmas. Oliver got dressed and sat in one of the locker rooms waiting for the private pre-game chalk session with Coach Mike. Coach Mike was a thin guy with a broad smile and a quiet nature off the ice. Come game time, he was more expansive. He'd stand atop the bench during games and bark abrupt commands to his roster. When the game wasn't going well, Coach would jam his hands deep into his pants pockets and pull his ball cap low over his eyes. If the game turned exceptionally ugly, Mike would hurl his cap at anything inanimate. He treated the kids well, though, and at this point in the season they considered his every sentence to be gospel.

My wife and I were waiting in one of the two rinks in the Southern Ice facility there in the Nashville suburbs. The building was a modern, flat skating factory tucked away by a shopping mall amidst acres of brand-new brick homes. The area had the look of any upper-middle-class suburb in the heartland of America: black lampposts, uniform lawns, 3,500-square-foot neo-colonial homes with brick fronts and heavily gabled roofs, dinky trees.

We got Oliver's skates sharpened at the immense pro shop. We drank better-than-average coffee from the gleaming concession stand. The hallways were filled with tables displaying items for a silent auction designed to raise funds for the local youth hockey programs. You could bid on pucks signed by NHL stars, a small guitar autographed by Vince Gill and Amy Grant, even a Predators mini-bike. This was a moneyed suburb. Oh, and just to remind you that you were in Baptist country, you could also bid on a series of *Veggie Tales Bible Story* DVDs. (For those unfamiliar with *Veggie Tales*, it's a cartoon series created by people who seem to think that scripture is more palatable to first-graders if, say, Noah is a talking, two-dimensional artichoke.)

The Nashville rinks—there were two—both featured giant banners that promoted the big-league franchise. Faith Hill's face was on one of the banners, complete with a faux black eye and an equally fake missing tooth. She grinned at the camera. Even with the bruises and rotten dental work, Faith was *still* a GLM. The place gleamed. Spectators stood or sat on long, brilliant aluminum benches, warmed by the radiant heaters that hung overhead. Under the ice, the paint denoting the red line, blue lines, goal lines, and circles was fresh. The glass above the boards seemed completely free of marks and scratches; you could actually see the game perfectly.

The games ahead of ours all had run late. The 4 p.m. face-off wouldn't come until at least 4:30. As my wife and I made small talk with some of the other hockey parents from Indy, we heard a crack, a whistle, and a gasp from the crowd watching the game that was in progress.

We spun toward the ice. A child, a Pee Wee, eleven or twelve years old, was lying in the middle of the ice and writhing in pain. Everyone was utterly silent for a full minute until a murmur ran through the crowd. The sound we'd all heard wasn't right, it wasn't good, it wasn't, well, *normal*. Two adult men stepped tentatively onto the ice and, upon reaching the child, leaned over him, asking him questions and prodding him gently. The refs marshalled boys from both teams away from the accident scene and herded them toward their respective benches. A man in a suit and tie shuffled onto the ice from the opposite side of the rink and slid his wing tips toward the kid. Parent? Doctor? We couldn't tell.

News rocketed through the group. An assistant coach from Memphis told us that the child who was hurt was a Nashville local and that EMTs were on the way, sirens wailing. The adults on the ice hoisted the boy to his feet. Both teams hammered their sticks on the ice or the boards in rhythm—it was the only way a hockey player in full pads and gloves was able to applaud. The boy set one skate on the ice gingerly as the adults who shouldered him lifted his feet up as best they could. The injured kid kept his right foot off the ice, grimacing as the adults hauled him toward the exit and a waiting ambulance.

Mr. S., father of Oliver's teammate Danny and two other hockey-playing boys, spoke knowingly aloud but to no one in particular: "That child's got a broken leg."

My wife rubbed her temples.

"That sound—the way he bent up—happened to my oldest once a few years back. That child's got a broken leg."

91

My wife covered her eyes with her right hand.

"It's okay," I told her. "Checking isn't allowed in Oliver's league."

My dear, sweet, patient, and loving wife told me to shut up.

Time-Out: BREAKING STUFF

Two years later, when Oliver was playing in a checking league for a Pee Wee travel team, Amy got the firsthand experience of watching her own kid break something. Early in the first period of the second game on a Saturday afternoon, Oliver, still a defenseman, was charging toward an offensive player from Carmel, Indiana—a town in the 'burbs just north of Indianapolis. The Carmelite had the puck, and Oliver meant to either take the disc or knock the kid over. Oliver came in for the check and the other kid ducked low.

Amy said later that she wasn't sure what the kid from Carmel was trying to do. Was he trying to get low enough so that Oliver would flip clean over him? Was he just trying to keep his vital organs further away from the advancing monster that was flying toward him?

Either way, the strategy didn't work. Oliver and the kid from Carmel slammed into one another at top speed. Upon impact, Ollie did what he'd been trained to do—explode into the opponent and skate through the check. You don't try to slow down or, even worse, back out—this always led to an injury. The opposing kid left the ice, skates akimbo as he landed on his back and slid into the boards with a resounding boom. Oliver had delivered a massive hit to a kid who outweighed him by thirty pounds.

Oliver's extended right thumb, however, had made contact with the kid's facemask as the offensive player had ducked, and the impact had traveled down the fully developed digit until it found a soft spot—a plate-like, undeveloped bone in the hand just below the bottom knuckle of Oliver's thumb. The little plate snapped and sent an electric bolt of "YOWZA!" out to the tips of Ollie's digits and back toward his funny bone, then settled into a dull, persistent ache that radiated over the back of his hand.

Ollie skated over to the bench and sat down. He stuck his right hand under his left armpit. He bent forward, eyes welling with tears. "Are you okay?" asked his coach.

"Fine," said Ollie bravely.

Oliver played the next two periods with a broken hand. He laid off the hits and handled his stick only with his left hand, but he managed to stop a few breakaways as he and his mates lost to the team from Carmel by a final of 6–2.

After the game, his coaches examined Ollie's hand. They prodded it and nudged it and wiggled Oliver's thumb. He winced now and again, but the initial pain seemed to have subsided quite a bit. The area around the base of Ollie's thumb was swollen, but the coaches and my wife were debating the condition of Ollie's hand. Some thought it might be a simple sprain. One of the assistants, a guy named Matt who hailed from New England, shook his head.

"I betcha gaht a break thayuh," he said.

Amy was, of course, upset. She wasn't, however, positive that anything was broken. The kid said he felt better and was able to handle stuff—he could pick up his bag, his stick, his helmet with the help of the opposable thumb on his right hand. She decided to wait until morning and see how the kid felt. She iced the child down and called me—I was in Los Angeles on business when all of this transpired.

The next morning, the swelling around Ollie's thumb had all but disappeared. Amy took his right thumb and moved it slightly forward. Oliver said brightly, "Feels okay!" She moved it from side to side. The kid was smiling.

Amy moved the child's thumb a millimeter back away from the palm.

YOWZA.

Ollie let out a yelp. Amy called the doctor.

The x-rays showed a small crack in the undeveloped plate that supported Ollie's right thumb, a part of his bone structure that had yet to mature. The physician at the immediate care center showed the x-rays to Ollie and his mom and told Oliver he was probably going to be fitted for a cast.

Oliver asked if he could play hockey next weekend.

"Honey," said the doc, a chubby African-American woman, "you won't be playing hockey for at least another month."

Oliver burst into tears.

Amy did some research and found a local pediatrician who specialized in youth sports injuries. He gave Ollie a better prognosis: There would be a cast, yeah, but with the proper rest and a little bit of caution, Ollie might be able to play, plaster and all, come state tournament time two weeks down the road. The doc fitted Ollie's cast around the butt of a hockey stick that the physician just happened to have lying around in his office and turned the kid loose.

Ollie took a week off from hockey. By the end of day three he was bouncing off the walls—an atomic ball of hockey energy that wasn't allowed to check or skate or shoot. During the second week of recovery, Ollie skated with his team wearing an adult glove over his right hand and a standard youth glove on his left.

He looked strangely asymmetrical. Somebody noted that when he was outfitted in his gear, the kid kind of looked like the bastard son of a Star Wars stormtrooper and a fiddler crab.

His coach pointed to Ollie's right hand. "Don't hit anybody with that thing," he cautioned.

Ollie just smiled.

Ollie played with his team, ran with his team, did everything with his team with a broken mitt. The only time the cast slowed him down was when he wanted to go swimming with the rest of the travel team and had to sit on the edge of a hotel pool, glumly watching his teammates try to drown each other in the name of fun.

Ollie played tournament hockey that year with the cast on his right hand. He played brilliantly for two games, stopping opposing forwards at every turn and blasting in a goal himself, bum wing and all. Before the third game of the double elimination tourney, our team still alive for a shot at glory with one loss and a win, the kids and parents had gone to Wendy's for a bite. As luck would have it, so did the coach of the team we'd face next, the Fort Wayne Komets.

I happened to overhear the Fort Wayne chief ("Happened to overhear?" Okay, I was tailing the guy the way the paparazzi used to stalk Lady Di) commiserate with the refs right before the face-off. "Hey," said Coach Concerned, "it's no difference to us, but I'm pretty sure the rules state that a kid with a hard cast has to sit. I think that's the rule. Of course, it's your call."

Cute. "Yeah, ref, it doesn't make a bit of difference to us, but I thought I'd bring it up anyway. Just in case, y'know, one of their largest kids should happen to be disqualified."

During warm-ups the refs called Ollie over to the scorer's box. Coaches and refs huddled as Ollie pulled off one glove and showed everyone the cast. A ref squeezed it. Studied it. Looked at the Fort Wayne coach. Spit on the ice.

"It ain't plaster. It's fiberglass. The kid plays."

The ref skated away. Coach Concerned hurled his clipboard to the floor. Apparently, the whole thing did make a difference to somebody. I made a note to thank Ollie's doctor for knowing exactly what materials were legal in youth hockey.

Five weeks later, when the cast came off, Ollie's hand was as good as new. His mom wasn't happy, though. She'd spent a month wrapping the kid's arm up in plastic every time he wanted a shower, she'd spent a month transcribing his homework from his left-handed scrawl into something legible, and after all of that extra mothering, we owed the various magicians who had healed our little Gretzky about five hundred bucks that our insurance didn't cover.

He didn't know it, but Junior had spent a month wearing the new front door to our house on his right hand.

RESUME PLAY

Nobody broke anything the year our boy played with the Indy Junior Ice Squirt A team. The only thing that got broken in Nashville for the Junior Ice was morale.

As a result of the delays—including the stoppage in play for the injury time-out—it was 4:45, a full forty-five minutes late, before the puck was finally dropped for the first game between our Indy Junior Ice Squirt A team and The Southern Ice Lightning Squirt A's from Nashville.

At 4:47, every parent from Indy held the opinion that the fix was in.

It sounds like absolute bull, an utter rationalization, but with God as my witness, I tell you this: Yours truly absolutely never complains about the officials in youth hockey games. The striped shirts can range in age from sixteen to sixty, and theirs is a job rewarded only with epithets, criticism, and the occasional threatening gesture. I feel for these men and women who carry the whistles and hear the insults.

The refs in Nashville—it seemed to me—were determined that only youth hockey teams from Nashville would make it to the championship round. Goals were waved off when the visitors scored. The Nashville kids were awarded penalty shots. There was always a child in the penalty box, and that child never wore a Lightning jersey.

Angry catcalls came up from the Indy crowd: "Homer! Homer! Homer!" (Homer (*n*): an official who by deed or action makes it clear that he is pulling for the home team by calling a game in its favor with the sole intent of inflicting a loss on our precious little children on the visiting team after we spent all this money on ... Well, you get the picture.)

I could feel the acid rising in my guts. When Oliver had first been elevated to the rank of All-Star the previous season, my reactions during the games were pretty limited. I cheered when somebody scored or a goalkeeper made a terrific save, but my emotions were always in check. Now, with Ollie wearing the letter "A" on his jersey, an assistant captain on a travel team, I was more of a screamer. Not quite enough to be classified as a Yelling Man yet, but ...

I was getting more and more torqued up with each game. My patter took the form of a long bellow, jawing directions at my kid with a furious intensity. My mantra had become "Think, Ollie, think!" I yelled that at least a dozen times per period.

I was starting to become concerned about my reactions. I was way too into this. Was I becoming the very overzealous jerk that

I'd so often criticized privately? Was I living vicariously through Ollie? Did I expect this to pan out into a college scholarship? A pro career? The kid was only ten years old. How close was I to morphing into Robert Duvall in *The Great Santini?*

I couldn't help it. The game wasn't being officiated properly. I was pissed. Ollie was pissed. Ollie had spent half the game in the penalty box. I was spending an entire afternoon knee-deep in the politics of youth hockey, as if any of this mattered at all. My blood pressure must have been rising. Between my barely muted rage and the forty grams of cholesterol I'd sucked out of my drive-thru Breakfast Croissanamuffin, I'd be lucky to see nightfall without having a ventricle explode.

Nashville. What the hell was going on here in Nashville?

Sometimes, folks, your child's team will be better than the other child's team. And sometimes, folks, your guys will simply be worse.

And on certain rare occasions, people actually rig a game involving ten-year-olds.

I like to think of myself as a rational guy, a guy who'd consider the subjective nature of whatever I'm seeing. Obviously, since it's my little bundle of DNA that's getting thumped out there, I'm going to naturally, and probably incorrectly, assume that he's being treated unfairly. I'm his dad. I'm *supposed* to feel that way. As an Intelligent Man of the New Millennium, I'm also supposed to recognize that an objective take on the situation is impossible.

While I was trying to sort things out, trying to determine if there was any difference at all between what I was seeing and what I *thought* I was seeing, my wife tugged at my sleeve.

"Honey," Amy queried, "does it seem right to you that we're losing to this Nashville team?" I looked at her. Her brow was knitted.

"What do you mean?" I ventured slowly.

"Well, I've seen the puck go in their goal about four or five times, and we're losing by three to one."

"No," I said. "It's not right that we're losing to this Nashville team."

After the game, I made my way to the locker room. No after-the-game speech today. Coach Mike sat in a corner of the locker room while the kids undressed in silence. The brim of his hat was pulled low over his eyes.

Mike tipped his cap back. He stood and jammed his hands into his pockets.

"Guys," said Mike, "count that one as a win. We got suckered."

Mike left the locker room.

It occurred to me that Mike had been oddly quiet during most of the Nashville debacle. Later, I found out he didn't want to pipe up for fear that he'd saddle the kids with even more penalty minutes.

I knelt in front of Oliver. How do you explain something like this—adults appearing to rig a ten-year-old's hockey game?

"Tough loss," I said.

Oliver grinned at me. "We didn't lose. We got suckered."

"Really?"

"Yeah. We were better, so the refs just didn't play fair."

Alright then. As a parent, I was clearly over-thinking this little moral lesson. Oliver had processed the situation correctly. Sometimes, kiddo, life just ain't fair. No grand explanation from dear old dad was needed here. The coach told him what was happening in its simplest form, and the boy understood. Glad you got it, son. Sorry.

Things got uglier. Word spread through the rink: A Mite team from Indy had tied two other teams for a spot in a championship game; one was a local squad. Names had been placed in a hat as a tiebreaker, and—the Nashville team got the draw.

By Sunday afternoon, Nashville teams were playing against Nashville teams for each championship trophy.

We played our remaining games, losing a squeaker to Baton Rouge, getting pounded by Nashville again (naturally), and thumping the kids from Memphis. The refs' calls were equitable when both teams on the ice had zero chance of playing the local kids in the final round. We were finished with youth hockey by 2 p.m. Nashville time and decided to take a look at Music City in all its beer-soaked glory. It was time to put the Southern Ice Lightning Invitational behind us. We wouldn't be playing for any glory on Sunday, so the rest of the weekend was ours to spend freely.

Time-Out: REFS

Okay, so the refs in Nashville had a mission—but honestly, in my heart of hearts, I believe those gents were the exception.

Pity the poor ref. The youth hockey ref takes home a minimum wage stipend for suffering heckling no boxer has ever endured.

A lot of refs are coaches who simply love ice hockey or older kids who are picking up a couple of bucks between games. And what do they get for their efforts besides a thin check on Friday? Shouts and catcalls and whistles and boos and swearing and cussing—and all from some child's sainted mother. This is what rings through the ears of the lonely zebra who's just flagged little Num-Nums for tripping some kid with his hockey stick. Sure,

Num-Nums hooked another kid's feet with the blade of his twig and pulled it like he was starting a lawnmower, but that was the team mom's child—and Num-Nums's mommy knows that Num-Nums can do no wrong.

The shouts rain down on every ref from both the stands and the bench, falling slowly early in the season, then growing to torrential status by the time the annual tournaments roll around in early March.

During one of Ollie's hockey games, a coach from Fort Wayne visiting the Junior Ice at Pan Am became so incensed that he dropped a few choice obscenities on a zebra. The ref was a dad and a coach himself who was officiating alongside his son. The ref didn't want the kids to hear the f-word, and he didn't necessarily want his son, the seventeen-year-old officiating alongside him, to hear it either, so he tossed the coach. Rightfully so.

On his way out, the coach climbed the boards to yell a few more choice words over the top of the glass. He was booed soundly by the parents of the Junior Ice. After the game was over and the Ice had beaten the Fort Wayne Komets five-zip, the offending coach stopped by the Junior Ice locker room. He announced to the kids: "YOU ALL PLAYED A GREAT GAME. DON'T KNOW WHY MY BUTT HURTS—CAN'T TELL WHETHER IT'S FROM THE REFS KICKIN' IT OR FROM YOU GUYS KICKIN' IT!"

I was helping Ollie out of his skates as the visiting coach walked out of the locker room. *Was that supposed to be some kind of an apology?* I wondered to myself.

Ollie looked at me. "That guy's nuts," he whispered.

I nodded. We never found out if the coach had any parting words for the referees that day.

RESUME PLAY

The drive into downtown Nashville from the 'burbs took about twenty minutes. We parked by the Ryman Auditorium, the venue that had once housed the Grand Ole Opry. We toured the Ryman, then wandered into a honky-tonk bar. The folks running the joint allowed Oliver to sit at a table with us as my wife and I split a beer. Oliver drank a soda as he sat transfixed by the bluegrass band on stage. There seemed to be more people playing than were sitting in the audience. Now and then the leader of the group, a grizzled old fart in a battered felt hat playing a glittering mandolin, would call another audience member up to the stage. Amy, Oliver, and I appeared to be the only people in the room who didn't know the band or have an instrument handy.

Guitar, fiddle, mandolin, dobro, banjo, bass—even the washboard player had a crack at singing lead:

"Met a gal and she' was thrillin'! Now I'm fulla penicillin!"

Oliver looked at me quizzically.

"I'll explain later," I told Oliver.

The old fart stepped back up to the mic. The band hung on a chord and repeated it as he mused aloud: "I cain't do this next verse. This is a family-type crowd!" He winked at Oliver and then sang:

"I like bacon, I like grits, I like gals with real biiiiig … feet."

Oliver cracked up.

We finished our drink and wandered the streets. We ate at a brewpub across the river from the stadium where the Tennessee Titans played. My wife ordered something on the menu called a "plantation salad." I laughed out loud. "That's the first time you've ever wanted anything that had the word 'plantation' attached," I noted.

The waitress looked at me sideways. My wife felt compelled to explain: "I *am* a Yankee. From Buffalo. That's in New York," she told our server. The waitress nodded, the gave Amy a blank stare. It was as if my wife had just told the waitress, "I am a Presbyterian," or, "I am a duckbill platypus." The waitress truly did not care. "And would y'all be wantin' sumthin' to drink with that salad?" My wife cringed. Yankees like Amy are aurally allergic to the Confederate drawl when it's not being sung over a rhythm section.

We finished dinner and headed away from the pub toward the Gaylord Arena, home ice of the NHL's Nashville Predators. The building, though obviously only a few years old, had the look of a spacecraft from a 1950s sci-fi film. I half expected a giant silver robot to take our tickets at the door.

We took our seats in the Gaylord, only a dozen rows below the ceiling. The view we had was similar to an overhead camera angle: The ice seemed to flatten out, and we could watch the plays develop from a real bird's-eye perspective. To my utter amazement, the building was packed with fans—and nearly half of them seemed to be wearing Detroit red.

Later that evening, I met a local hockey fan at the bar in our hotel. He was a Nashville native and a Predators season-ticket holder, still wearing his bronze and blue Nashville jersey. He told me that the team, in the midst of another losing season, had actually seen disappointing attendance of late—except for their matchups with the Red Wings. The Saturn auto plant in nearby Spring Hill had drawn hundreds of transplants from the Detroit area. As more and more Saturns were built, more and more GM workers fled Motown for the Sun Belt, and they donned the red and white when the Wings came to the Gaylord.

The scoreboard in the Gaylord was a massive box that hung from the ceiling over center ice. Four jumbo TV screens on the box flashed replays, graphics, jokes about the opponent, and an occasional live look at the house organist, a skinny kid who looked to be about nineteen wearing thick glasses and a cowboy hat. Fire shot out from the top of the suspended scoreboard to punctuate certain sound effects that the keyboard player had at his command.

At one point, the board flashed some footage of the Red Wings' bench. It wasn't the actual scene, though—we were treated to a long panning shot of a group of toothless old geezers wearing Detroit gear and waving canes. This was followed by a gag about the Wings' upcoming endorsement deal with Viagra. Yes, that season the Red Wings were old guys by NHL standards, but they were still beating the Predators 3–0 at this point.

When the Predators finally scored, the Gaylord rolled tape of country singer Tim McGraw on the scoreboard. He was wearing what seemed to be the official uniform of the Preds fan: a blue and bronze jersey with a black cowboy hat. "I like it! I love it!" he wailed into a studio microphone somewhere in Nashville. The Preds were losing. The management of the Gaylord took no notice. The presentation remained big, loud, and glitzy.

The Predators' mascot ran up and down the aisles. His name was "Gnash" (Get it? Predators? Sabre-teeth? Nashville? Gnash?), and he looked suspiciously like Boomer, the NBA mascot for the Indiana Pacers.

Boomer was—well, what the hell was Boomer?—a cat, maybe, or somebody's interpretation of a cat after ingesting a sandwich topped with psychedelic mushrooms. Boomer had a blue face and yellow whiskers, and he dunked baskets off a mini-trampoline. In recent seasons, Boomer had been joined on the court by Bowser, a kind of cartoon dog who looked like somebody's undead pet from the movie *Beetlejuice*. Neither Bowser nor Boomer had the aggressive, almost mean-spirited energy of Gnash.

Gnash was some sort of athletic-looking blue feline with an oversized cartoon head and the calm, reserved demeanor of somebody who'd just swallowed thirty capsules of trucker speed. He had entered the arena just before the national anthem by sliding down a rope from the ceiling. He'd spent most of the game harassing Red Wings fans, even setting up a prank where a Wings fan received a funnel full of beer down the front of his pants. I was surprised Gnash didn't spend most of his time getting his ass kicked by a few of the Motor City refugees he was annoying.

On the other hand, who cared? Revenge was on the scoreboard. Detroit was winning big. The Gaylord began to empty halfway through the third period.

I'd been profoundly impressed by the hockey knowledge that this crowd seemed to bring to the game. They knew the obvious stuff, sure—cheer for a great save in the net, chant "fight" when somebody drops his gloves—but they also knew to cheer when the Preds iced the puck during a Wings' power play. (If you're confused by the phrase "iced the puck during a Wings power play," don't worry—everything gets explained before the end of the book.) Suffice to say that these hillbilly folk were cheering for the right stuff while watching the National Sport of Canada.

Hillbilly music and ice hockey. How in the world had these two things been twisted together? The game was gaining popularity in the South. More northerners had moved to warmer climates, and they'd brought a love of cold-weather sports with them. The Poles brought kielbasa and the Germans gave us the Christmas tree— why shouldn't a Chicagoan drag a love for the frozen pond with him when emigrating to Dallas? As soon as a southerner saw a hockey game live, he was hooked—hooked in a way that never would've happened if the same fan had only seen the game on ESPN.

Hockey doesn't translate to TV well. Focusing on the puck doesn't let you see the play develop; pull away from the close-up, and the casual viewer can't follow the puck at all. As a live sport, though, hockey has it going on—nearly continuous action interrupted by some occasional bloodletting. This is why ratings for hockey on TV remain weak, but attendance at a lot of minor-league games in the South has gone through the roof. What else is there to do in Shreveport when it isn't baseball season?

A friend had told me about a situation in Pensacola, Florida. The local coffers couldn't fund both a minor-league hockey team and an Arena Football League franchise. Both teams had established themselves as a fairly decent draw for local sports fans, but the town could support only one. They'd put the decision to a vote—and hockey had won the referendum. (By the way, the team is named the Pensacola Ice Pilots. Not real exciting, but not a reference to hurricanes, either.)

We waited until the final buzzer sounded to leave the Gaylord. Nearly all of the parents and kids from Indy sitting beside us waited for the end of the game, as well. As the crowd trudged out of the rink, Detroit fans in their red and white jerseys called to one another and to Oliver. Oliver raised his hands above his head and yelled back. The halls of the Gaylord rang with the echoes of a thousand Yankee accents as all the Michigan natives headed back to their new homes in the cradle of the old Confederacy. The geese had flown south, but this time they were staying.

The drive home from Nashville was an all-day affair. We'd pulled off of I-65 north to try a scenic route through Kentucky that took us right past Lincoln's birthplace. The hills rolled away from us in every direction, gentle and still a bit green in winter.

We stopped at a gas and convenience store to see if we could find an ATM. A customer in the store—an older lady without her dentures—gave us directions.

"Y'all be wantin' a cash machine y'all gonna have t'be down the road ta four mile marker or uppin the village ta Hodgenville."

I couldn't make head or tail of what she was saying. The accent and the dental trouble turned her T's into D's and her vowels into mud. Amy stepped in and asked the woman to write down her directions. Oliver trailed me out of the store while Amy and the woman commiserated.

When Amy emerged from the store and got in the car, Oliver and I were waiting with the motor running. She laughed. "I've never seen you two leave anywhere so quick!"

"The lady with no teeth freaked me out!" said Oliver.

"Be nice, now," cautioned Amy. "I have a feeling that lady was very poor."

I said nothing. Rolling hills soothed my soul—rolling gums didn't. But Oliver didn't need to hear that, and Amy would've killed me for cracking wise at that point. We drove on to Abraham Lincoln's birthplace, just south of Hodgenville and the elusive ATM. At the top of a low knob stood a granite monument, fronted by columns and fifty-six granite steps leading down to the bottom of the hill. We climbed the steps and entered the monument. We knew what was inside, but the effect was still surprising: Inside this grand edifice was Lincoln's first home, a one-room cabin, perfectly preserved.

The exterior building allowed about four feet of space around the perimeter of the cabin inside. You could walk clear around the ancient wooden structure, peer into the windows—you couldn't touch it, mind you, but you were close enough to smell it. A family of Hindu tourists leaned over the ropes that blocked access to the cabin, hoping to see something through the single window or the door, something more than just four bare walls and a fireplace.

The monument was mind-boggling. Just think of it, especially as a parent: Can you imagine future generations holding you or your child in this kind of regard? Suppose Junior grew up to end the Galactic Civil War and free the Martian slaves held in captivity on distant Io, moon of Jupiter! Would the people of Unified Earth encase the kid's childhood home in synthetic marble? "Witness the simple and rustic vinyl-sided two-and-a-half-bath, three-bedroom dwelling of our Great Leader as a boy! Imagine the hardship of day-to-day life in the twenty-first century—what toil must have been involved to operate the gravity flush toilet and the propane grill!" How in the world would you sell the very *idea* of the monument to the neighborhood association?

The Hindus took our picture. We took pictures of the Hindus. We saw the spring where Abe took his first drink of water. We went home to our simple and rustic vinyl-sided two-and-a-half-bath, three-bedroom cabin.

JANUARY—1st PERIOD

New Year's passed pleasantly enough. Amy decided to throw a party for Oliver, a sleepover at our place with eight of Ollie's closest friends attending. The madness had its method: One night of chaos meant that every one of those kids' parents might feel obligated to extend a sleepover invitation to Ollie in return. My wife had the ability to wrangle free babysitting any time she needed it.

The parents didn't drop and run, either. We'd stocked the bar well enough so that the moms and dads had reason to stay and converse.

Donna and Al rolled up with their three kids. Alex, Brian, and five-year-old Matthew were spending the night. None of the three had any interest in hockey, except for perhaps Matt, who seemed to enjoy simply running into things.

Next in were Zack and his mom and dad, Bob and Cara. Zack was a winger with a legendary temper. The next group included Jeremy, Ollie's buddy on defense, and his folks, Jenny and Pete.

Jenny and Pete were from Buffalo, just like Amy. They always had a cooler stocked full of summer sausage and cheeses, and Pete enjoyed a cold one as much as I did—and wasn't ashamed of it, either. Pete always wore a bandana on his head and never, ever yelled during the game. He'd pace along the boards, stop, watch, pace, shake his head, and continue. His wife, Jenny, picked a spot in the stands and stayed there. She started yelling at the face-off and never stopped until the last buzzer sounded. Nothing critical though, always encouraging. We liked both of them immensely.

Cara and Bob were a similar couple. Bob was a quiet guy, and when Cara got rolling, you knew why: The woman had a hundred stories to tell. Cara regaled us all with tales of her redneck family in Bradenton, Florida. Her dad and his "Angry Geezer Neighbor" had been feuding for years, and apparently had resorted to some pretty serious vandalism lately: spinning vehicular doughnuts in one another's yards, splattering each other's houses with paintball pellets, and so on. When Cara had flown down to Bradenton to see her folks for the holidays, she had stepped outside while Angry Geezer Neighbor was getting his mail. Geezer had dropped his pants and flipped Cara the digit. Cara yelled some choice obscenities at the old coot and the racket caused one of her relatives to investigate. Cara's kin had attempted to run over Geezer with a Ford pickup, but, alas, had failed. According to Cara, the cops in Bradenton thought this behavior was entertaining as hell and never arrested anybody for fear of stopping the show.

As Cara kept rapping, Donna and Al raised their eyebrows skeptically. Bob made eye contact and nodded sincerely. His wife wasn't lying.

To me, this was the most satisfying part of Ollie's love affair with hockey. I was a media geek, Amy was a preschool teacher at a Montesorri academy. In any other universe besides youth travel hockey, we would never have met Zack's mom and dad. They lived in another part of town and manufactured sportswear apparel. Our paths probably never would have crossed had it not been for the Junior Ice.

We spent a few hours engaged in the time-honored tradition of shooting the bull. The kids ran wild through the house, splitting themselves into two warring nations and maneuvering through hostile territories, like the guest bedroom and the garage. A few more moms and dads wandered in and out, dropping kids and draining beers. It was almost 10 p.m. when young Matt, his parents long gone on a romantic night on the town without children, announced to the adults in a loud, albeit slow, voice: "Are you guys aware that at 7 p.m. I have to go home and feed my gecko?"

Had the kid not been five, we would've been waiting for the punchline to a very dirty joke.

Nobody got hurt, nobody broke anything, and as the night drifted on and every last guardian but Amy and I had wandered into the darkness, we started to get to know Ollie's teammates. It's funny, but you imprint personalities on kids based on what you know of their folks. If you knew Bob, you'd expect Zack to be shy, if you knew Cara, you'd figure Zack to be expansive. Zack was somewhere in the middle, grinning and good natured but ready to give anybody in authority what for. Jeremy was a gamer, a focused kid ready to pitch in with the chores. Ollie— well, Ollie was the cheerleader, and his endless patter surely had a lot to do with the other kids handing him the role of assistant captain on the team.

Ollie would raise his hands to the Junior Ice parents in the stands during a stoppage in play, always asking for A LITTLE MORE NOISE, PEOPLE! Ollie led the chants by the goal before the game and banged his stick the hardest when an injured opponent finally struggled to his feet. But Ollie also spent a lot of time in the pen for "checking in a non-checking league"—his enthusiasm occasionally caused him some grief.

On New Year's Day the snow began again. A constant snowpack had been a rarity in Indiana since my family had moved here, but this winter promised to be a season that reminded Amy of her childhood home back in Buffalo. Saturday saw us back on I-74, leaving our house at 5:30 a.m. in the frosty darkness for two games in Cincinnati.

The drive from Indianapolis to Cincinnati takes about two hours. We'd given ourselves just enough time to make the game—maybe with Ollie's laces a bit loose, mind you, but we'd make it. I leaned into the accelerator, and my dinky Saturn whined and went plunging toward the dawn. Snow covered the low hills and gullies, and the early light cast everything in a deep blue.

There are three kinds of terrain in the Hoosier state: flat, not quite flat, and the "Uplands." The flat part breeds industrial farms and big racetracks. The Uplands start where the ancient glaciers stopped, running in two strips that bracket the towns just south of Indianapolis in a funky "U" that spreads south and widens toward the Ohio River.

We passed the exit for Milan, Indiana, on I-74 East. Milan was the town with the underdog high school basketball team that had won the state championships in the 1950s and inspired the movie *Hoosiers*. In the movie, the name of the town had been changed to Hickory and the coach looked a lot like Gene Hackman. In real life, the kid who sank the winning bucket—Bobby Plump—grew up and bought a bar in Indy called Plump's Last Shot, and the days of a single state-wide champion had long since passed. The small towns now played other small towns, and the big cities played each other.

The death of the old system, the idea of multiple championships in different classes instead of a single winner-take-all tourney, had caused a firestorm of controversy in Indiana. The newspapers covered it. The local news broadcasts were filled with it. The story went on for months. The man who owned Plump's Last Shot was dead set against it. His side lost. His side remains upset to this day. Basketball could make this much news only in the state of Indiana.

Basketball was Indiana's sport. Hockey belonged to Michigan, Minnesota, the Empire State—not the home of Indiana University, Purdue, and the Butler Bulldogs in Indianapolis. Roundball was the Hoosier tradition. Puck was never played by anybody named Bird. It didn't even matter that Wayne Gretzky had started his professional career in Indianapolis—most folks were only dimly aware that the Great One had even driven through the city, much less played there, albeit briefly.

Hockey is something that's virtually unknown to about 80 percent of the Hoosier state. When the NHL decided to cancel an entire season because of a salary dispute between players and management, I bet less than a quarter of the Hoosier state even noticed. To most folks at the Crossroads, hockey is a thirty-five-mile-per-hour boxing match played by guys with accents like Bob and Doug McKenzie or Inspector Clouseau, a mysterious game full of circles and lines that look more like an alien landing field than a competitive surface.

How ya figure, eh? The game kind of looks like basketball on skates, right? Five guys shooting and rebounding, albeit with a goalie blocking the net—the plays unwind in a similar pattern to hoops, oui? And wasn't it our Americanski hockey-playin' fellers who beat those damn commie bastard Soviets in the Olympics back in '80? Hoosiers always dig a good pinko butt-whuppin', no matter what the decade! Why don't we love this sport?

Well, for one thing, Indiana usually doesn't have those Minnesotan/New England-style deep-freezes from Halloween to April Fool's Day. Every November, the local weatherman predicts, "Ooh, another *terrible Indiana winter* is just around the corner ..."

Nope. Not so much.

Yeah, it snows, yeah, it gets cold—but our home here in Indiano-place ain't no St. Paul, baby. You can't skate on the pond out back save for a couple odd weeks in January. Ice hockey is big in Canada *because there's lots of ice in Canada.*

I hear the counterpoint: "Then explain how come ya had yer NHL in yer Southern states, pal?"

Well, like I said before—the rust belt is being emptied. Hockey country is full of dark and empty factories overrun by weeds and dust. All those fans have been moving south, south where football is king and baseball usually runs a close second, south to Texas and Florida and Arizona. Suddenly, right around the turn of the millennium, hockey teams began magically appearing in the Sun Belt.

We've never had the NHL in Indy, but we have had big-league hockey. The Indianapolis Racers, a World Hockey Association franchise that existed in the Hoosier capital from 1974 to 1978, fielded a team at Market Square Arena that employed a seventeen-year-old kid named Wayne Gretzky. Number 99 played his first eight professional games in Indy, racking three goals and three assists before shuffling off to Edmonton and making hockey history. As I've mentioned, his number, retired in 1999, hangs in the rafters at Pepsi Coliseum. The World Hockey Association was eventually absorbed by the NHL.

Yes, boys and girls, once upon a time Hall of Famers skated in

Indy. Even Gordie Howe and Bobby Hull took the ice at Market Square Arena just a few blocks from the very heart of the city of Indianapolis. That's why, though the sport has faded, though the NHL has locked and punched and bullied itself out of true national popularity, though Market Square Arena was imploded to make way for the glittering cathedral that the NBA's Indiana Pacers call their home court, there will always be at least some small amount of Hoosier interest in the stick and puck on the frozen pond.

As long as there are ten-year-olds who love hockey, hockey will not go away.

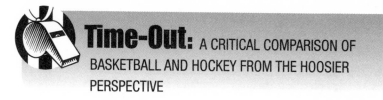

Time-Out: A CRITICAL COMPARISON OF BASKETBALL AND HOCKEY FROM THE HOOSIER PERSPECTIVE

Okay, so basketball is king in Indiana. We know. And the movies haven't helped. In my humble opinion, the best sports movies ever made are about ice hockey and basketball. They are, respectively, *Miracle* and *Hoosiers*. (Pretty handy for our little discussion here, yes?) *Hoosiers* is all Indiana, based loosely on the exploits of a tiny town in Indiana named Milan (pronounced MY-lin) that won the state championship during the old winner-take-all structure of the tourney in the 1950s. *Hoosiers* is 100 percent Hoosier. *Miracle*, the story of the 1980 U.S. Olympic hockey squad, is not. These two films are essentially the same—amateur sports organization loaded with fresh-faced young'uns wins ultimate title in the face of impossible odds by outsmarting much better squads. So, from a purely Hoosier perspective, which film is better? (Hint: Check the titles of both films before predicting the results.)

SETTING

Hoosiers: The fictional town of Hickory, Indiana (producers were afraid the public would confuse Milan, Indiana, with the fashion capital of Italy)

Miracle: Everywhere but Indiana

ADVANTAGE: *Hoosiers*

COACH

Hoosiers: Gene Hackman and his smartass grin

Miracle: Kurt Russell and his *Fargo* accent

ADVANTAGE: *Hoosiers*

TROUBLED TEEN

Hoosiers: One kid's dad is the town drunk and is played by Dennis Hopper.

Miracle: One kid's mom has passed away and is played by no one.

ADVANTAGE: *Hoosiers*

BREAKING DOWN THE EGOMANIACAL PLAYERS

Hoosiers: Coach benches the loudmouth

Miracle: Team loses game in half-assed fashion, does drills (now referred to as "Herbies" after Coach Herb Brooks) until rink manager turns out the lights

ADVANTAGE: *Miracle*

BIG WINNING SHOT IN REAL LIFE

Hoosiers: Bobby Plump

Miracle: Mike Eruzione

ADVANTAGE: *Hoosiers* ("Eruzione's Last Shot" is *not* the name of a bar today)

GEO-POLITICAL IMPACT

Hoosiers: Multi-class basketball sucks

Miracle: Communism sucks

ADVANTAGE: Tie

LOVE INTEREST

Hoosiers: Barbara Hershey

Miracle: Brooks's wife, played by vaguely familiar actress reminiscent of Carol Brady

ADVANTAGE: *Hoosiers*

OVERALL WINNER: *Hoosiers*—with a record of 4-2-1

Miracle might be more fun for you if your kid plays hockey, but *Hoosiers* is still the gold standard in the state of Indiana. Nonetheless, even here in the State of Roundball, as long as there are ten-year-olds who love hockey, hockey will not go away.

RESUME PLAY

The sun was coming up as we drove toward Cincinnati. Ohio was a dozen miles ahead. I surfed the radio dial looking for something interesting to listen to at 7:30 a.m. on a Saturday morning. The tuner stopped on a public radio station low on the dial. A Kentuckian DJ was hosting a free-form bluegrass show. He'd introduce every song three or four times, apparently forgetting halfway through every dedication that he'd already given you the title and the artist of the cut you were about to hear.

He played a gospel number for an eighty-year-old named Gertrude. He told the audience Gertrude a-told him he was doin' a fine job, and he was a-lucky he was a-wearin' a headset ta keep his haid from a-swellin'. I thought I'd driven into a black hole and was now somehow hearing a radio show from 1932. The radio blared a vocal, banjo, and bass arrangement called "I Feel the Tug."

I looked at the clock on my dashboard. We were going to make the face-off. The radio show was not going to improve.

I started counting and averaging the number of times the DJ mentioned the name of the artist for each cut. Three on the frontside, twice after. Usually he'd cut loose with something like, "Here's Billy Bob Cornliquor singin' that ol' fav-rit, 'Jesus Played Mah Fiddle and Now I Got the Stigmata Too,' by Billy Bob Redneck. Take it away, Billy Bob! Oh, did ah mention that this here Billy Bob Redneck song is a-goin' out to Gertrude?"

I was going to watch a youth travel hockey game within radio earshot of backwoods Appalachia. Only in America.

The Cincinnati Cyclones (on the plus side, the team wasn't named the Cincinnati Racial Unrest) had split their games that morning between two rinks roughly five minutes apart. Our first game against the 'Clones was in a heatless, battered facility that had all the charm of an Antarctic radar base.

The inside walls of the joint were covered with blackened dents, evidence that management really didn't give a damn if the kids were shooting pucks in the hallways. The blue and red lines under the ice had worn away around the edges. Dark stains marred the skating surface. The place had the stink of the worst rinks, an acrid funk that mirrored the Pepsi Coliseum on its creepiest day. It smelled of wet concrete and diesel exhaust, compounded by the fact that the Zamboni looked to be a real antique. Its paint was peeling, and it chugged a wispy gray smoke as it slid around the rink.

The first period was tight, but our team was down early on a "gimme" shot that our goalie Matt had somehow slept through. The child had been distracted by some action on his left, and the puck had dribbled into the net on his right. The Cyclones went through the celebratory motions, and Matt crumpled to the ice in dejection, head in his hands. Matt never missed the easy ones, and he saved 99 percent of the tough ones, too.

Grief for a goalie is downright biblical. Whether the goaltender is a first-year Mite or an NHL veteran with his name inscribed somewhere on Lord Stanley's cup, the reaction to missing an easy puck is universal. A twisting of the spine! A drop to the knees! A gnashing of teeth! The goalie beats his helmet with his mitt and slams his stick into the frozen pond. He shouts obscenities to the heavens with wild abandon, unconcerned about being grounded from his Playstation 2! Job himself would feel sorry for the poor bastard in the net who'd been caught napping. Had Matt had the strength in his ten-year-old arms to rend his garment, his Mom would've had plenty of sewing to do.

A second goal went in for Cincy. The Ice came within one, then fell back again. The final score came in at a disappointing 4-3, Cyclones. Pete, who was standing nearby, told me he'd heard that this game was the Cyclones' first win of the season. It was simply a passing observation, a statement made without malice— in fact, Pete gave a sad little chuckle when he told me. Neither he nor I knew that the simple fact that Pete had just relayed to me was the next-to-last straw on the back of somebody else's camel. There was unrest brewing among some of the hockey parents.

The second game would be played in a rink that was part of a larger complex. The place looked like a cross between a Chuck E. Cheese and a multi-use stadium, kind of a sports bar for kids. It had games you could play with tokens (which paid off in coupons you could exchange for some crappy prizes), an indoor soccer and lacrosse field, and a rock climbing wall.

We ate in the parking lot with Pete and Jenny's clan since the place didn't allow its patrons to eat any food that wasn't sold on the premises. Like good Buffalonians, Pete and Jenny and their kids were well prepared to eat their lunch outside in the cold. We all had coolers full of the standard meats and cheddar, and if we'd brought beer our little group might've been mistaken for an NFL tailgate gathering. Oliver and Jeremy smacked their hockey sticks against a wadded-up ball of black tape while Pete and Jenny's teenage daughter Nina sat in the front seat of the family's SUV listening to a Cincy pop station.

We talked of football and the few good sledding hills in Indy, we marveled at the fact that both Nina and her mom were fans of Santana. The air was chilly but the sun was warm, and the hilly suburbs of Cincinnati rose up around us in a way that felt almost sheltering. It was a good day to be a hockey dad and a good day to break bread with friends. I had a job, I had a happy family, I had two cars and a mortgage, I had a terrific house with a yard that was a royal pain in the ass, and I made more money than my dad ever had. My son was bright and healthy, and my wife loved me and I loved her—and I could still make her laugh. I had a moment of what must be the American answer to a Zen Buddhist's higher consciousness: five seconds of utter contentment. Fleeting, this nirvana.

We finished up and went inside.

I looked at my watch. It was time to round up the Squirts. Round two with the Cyclones was imminent.

It was about midway through the third and final period when it happened. The Junior Ice coaching staff decided to pull the goalie and send in an extra shooter to try and tie up a brutal 5-4 game. (The rule is that if nobody's serving time for a penalty, you can have six men on the ice. No matter if all six are crowded around your opponents' net. No matter if one is in goalie pads or not.) Parents here and there shrieked—*shrieked*—their disapproval. The angry chorus of catcalls grew in volume when Cincy very quickly put one in the open net, making the game a 6–4 affair.

Any inert fuel needs only a spark to burn. Drop a match into a can of gasoline, aim a magnifying glass properly toward some newspaper on a sunny day, call somebody's mama a slut, and the dung will get righteously twisted up in the fan. A tiny campfire can be swept along by the Santa Ana winds and become a raging inferno that devours the homes of the stars in Southern California. A small bit of oil on the Indianapolis Motor Speedway can send car careening into car and ruin the greatest spectacle in racing for a dozen drivers in seconds. So it is with the simmering human emotion of the youth sports parent, especially when our precious little children were going to lose a game to these rotten Ohioans after we'd spent all this money on … well, you get the picture.

Intermission: A FINE EXAMPLE OF POLITICS IN YOUTH SPORTS

Three days later, my wife started referring to the team as the Harper Valley Junior Ice.

"Harper Valley PTA" was a song by a country singer named Jeannie C. Riley from the late '60s or early '70s. I'd heard it on AM radio when I was a kid, and so had Amy, who remembered more about the song than I did. It was about some widow who wore mini-skirts and dated single guys. Her daughter came home one night with a note signed by the town elders cautioning the widow about her dress and behavior. Widow Badass responded by rolling into the PTA meeting and asked the good folk questions about their drinkin' and fightin' and birthin' them illegitimate babies, and then Billy Joe McAllister jumped off the Tallahatchie Bridge. Or something.

During the Tuesday night practice after the games in Cincy, my wife was pulled aside by a group of hockey parents who had kids on the Indy Junior Ice. The folks were upset about the coach. He wasn't teaching them right. We weren't winning games. He pulled the goalie. We weren't winning games. He didn't side with a parent in Fort Wayne when one of our moms had words with the opposing coach. We weren't winning games after we'd spent all this money on ...

(I wasn't at this particular practice. This is a good thing. I tend to be somewhat less than diplomatic in situations like this.)

Amy asked the group if anyone had thought of expressing her concerns to the coach directly.

Instead of answering—or looking sheepishly at their feet while Coach Emilio Estevez gazed at my wife gratefully, which is what would've happened if this had been a stupid *Mighty Ducks* movie—the parents simply proceeded to criticize each other.

No-we-didn't-talk-to-coach-about-it-*but* ...

Some parents sure did keep their kids up late when we went out on the road! *Some* parents sure made a point of using *every* hotel hot tub in their *skimpy* swimsuits! *Some* parents took their kids swimming right before a game! Shouldn't something be *done*?

Amy's back stiffened. First of all, what did the behavior of any grown person on the team have to do with the abilities of Coach Mike? Was he supposed to police the moms and dads? Set a dress code? Yeah, the coach could ask that a curfew be imposed—"Get 'em in bed by ten"—but had Mike actually had the lunatic chutzpah to criticize somebody's parenting or partnering skills, he would have been chased out of the league like he was the Frankenstein monster.

No, this wasn't *all* about the coach. It was also about a few select parents on the team. Amy even felt that one of the criticisms had been leveled directly at her. She often took Oliver swimming after a long car ride. If a pool was available at the hotel, they stretched out in it, game or no game.

Amy pointed and jawed. "Hey, I'll put my ass in a thong and swim all night if I want to. Nobody here can criticize anyone else as a parent!" She flipped a hand at everyone in the circle, one at a time. "I've seen *him* have more than a couple of belts. *She's* divorced—a few times? Twice?" The litany of sins continued.

Ken, the team manager, raised a hand. "Look," he said, "some people had concerns. We're just clearing the air."

Amy knew Ken to be a decent sort. "Then clear it with Coach Mike," she said. "We win, we lose, they're kids! Kids! You want an earlier curfew, we can talk about it. You want the kids not to swim before a game—well, I don't know. I don't know about that. They're kids. They're ten years old. Are you expecting them to go to the NHL or something?"

There were several nods.

Yes, some parents were expecting professional careers. Minor leagues or college scholarships at the very least.

Ken figured things out quickly. "Look," he said, "everybody's different, so everybody's kid is going to be different. I'm just a Hoosier hillbilly. The dads, the moms—we got doctors, lawyers, contractors, factory guys ..." He looked at Amy. "We got Ed ..." he shrugged. He meant me, morning drive DJ and freelance writer who somehow managed to wriggle ruminations about being a hockey dad into the local free hippie alternative weekly newspaper with the dirty personal ads in the back. I think I was a cipher to Ken most of the time.

"All I'm saying," Ken concluded, "is that maybe it's gonna take kids this different a little bit more time to gel."

Ken was trying to cover. A group of dissatisfied parents had tried to recruit our family into their group. They wanted us to pipe up and call out some other folks. At the very least, they wanted to spread some blame around when the Junior Ice got beat. It wasn't going to be a lousy play by *their* children that brought the team a mark in the "L" column—it was going to be a rotten coach or an inattentive mom.

Their children played travel hockey. That meant they were good, right? Best in their age group, right? Even though we were from Indiana—and yeah, the talent pool was thinner than in, say, Michigan or Minnesota—our kids were good, right? Too good to get beaten by those awful Cincinnati Cyclones, anyway …

And you know what? We didn't expect to get beaten by such a rotten team after we spent all this money on … Well, you get the picture.

Amy relayed the evening's events to me as soon as she and Oliver got home. She was upset and excited, waving her arms in frustration. "All some of those people want is a trophy! A bunch of them think they're paying for college right now!" She was furious; a raving thing.

I listened. What did any of us expect? What did I expect? A partial scholarship? A full one? A career in the minors, slogging from Toledo to Tulsa on a bus full of Canadians? Was the best kid from Indiana anywhere close to the worst kid who played travel hockey in Massachusetts? Did I expect to see the kid's name on Lord Stanley's Cup? A TV shot of me, proud papa in the stands wearing Ollie's jersey, the image beamed coast to coast on ABC?

Ridiculous. I didn't expect it.

But I thought about it at times.

I had started to change, subtly, but change nonetheless. I knew it wasn't *always* about the kids when my stomach began to roll and churn with each passing second of a game. There was a growing part of me that wanted my boy in there, in the thick of it, yeah, a little part of me wanted my kid to be a star. Was it wrong to feel cheated when the kids lost? Maybe. Probably. Definitely. C'mon. I kept my mouth shut. The kids were learning. They were having fun. Ollie said Coach Mike was the best coach he'd ever had. That was good enough for me.

But in my heart of hearts, in the darkest recesses of my soul, in the place in my gut that knew there'd one day be no finer man than this Oliver who was still just a little boy, I wanted everything for my kid. Everything. If he played defense for the Junior Ice, I wanted him to be the best damn defenseman the Corn Belt had ever seen. It was selfish, too. I wanted to be known as Oliver's dad, the man who'd raised his son to do great things.

What did I want? Really, secretly, deep down, what does any parent want? Everything. But you can't have everything. So—the name on the cup would do just fine. Or having our home encased in synthetic marble by the People of Unified Earth.

 Time-Out: YODA IN SKATES

The first Monday after New Year's, Oliver opened the mailbox to find his latest issue of *American Hockey* magazine, a publication geared for the youth hockey player (and consumer of expensive pads advertised in its pages). One of the featured teams in that issue was the Johnstown Warriors, an eight-and-under Mite squad. Oliver asked me excitedly, "Do you think I would've been on this team if we still lived in Johnstown when I was eight?"

I looked at the photo of the Warriors. "Yeah," I said. "Did you read the caption under the picture?"

Oliver read it out loud: "With many of the players returning from a winless season, the Warriors worked together as a team to win the Mite A Division of the Pittsburgh Amateur Hockey League. Not only did they win the division, the Warriors were undefeated."

"You see?" I asked, ready to dispense wisdom that would've made Ward Cleaver proud. "They kept trying, and last season they were perfect."

Oliver held the magazine gingerly, as awestruck as if he'd just been handed the Gutenberg Bible or his first *Playboy*. "No, Dad—that's *better* than perfect."

Better than perfect? Sometimes I wasn't sure if was raising Bobby Orr or the Dalai Lama. What kind of enlightened state allowed the condition of "Better than perfect"? Nonetheless, I wasn't going to contradict the kid. Amy had seen a rift developing among the parents and had said what she'd hoped would help those folks see the light. If they hadn't, no matter; Amy would recruit whoever she could to help her cheer and clap and call out encouraging words even if the Junior Ice was losing a game by four thousand goals. Maybe if that rift extended to the locker room, my boy could use some of his mom's smarts.

JANUARY—2ⁿᵈ PERIOD

Right after New Year's, I caught the flu—and a brutal case at that. I refused to let a little thing like the flu slow me down. I went to work. I struggled. Everybody else at work had gotten a flu shot. I hadn't. I refused to admit defeat to a few ugly microbes wreaking havoc on my immune system. The DJ and freelance writer would not be defeated by a little thing like bubonic plague.

In truth, I was a mess. My tonsils felt like I'd gargled with sandpaper. Aches shot down the backs of my legs. My back felt as if someone had pressed sheets of aluminum foil between the vertebrae. My eyes burned in the faintest of light, and a hundred fingers seemed to squeeze at the base of my skull. Through Thursday and Friday I muddled on—and on Saturday, I pulled my sorry ass together for a Junior Ice doubleheader against the Decatur Flames at one of our home rinks.

Most junkies and addicts have a rock-bottom point that precludes further behavior: The gambler runs out of cash, the drunk goes comatose, the smackhead expires. Sports junkies have no such luck. There's always a game someplace.

The rink we were playing in that Saturday was in Greenwood, just south of Indianapolis. It was a state-funded joint called Perry Park, and it had a playground and a swimming pool with numerous complex slides for warmer weather. It was nice a place, worn but with a friendly vibe. It didn't have a pro shop, but it did have some decent concessions and a few heaters for the spectators in the actual rink.

It also had been spared by the twisters.

On a warm afternoon the previous September, the tornado sirens that covered central Indiana had all gone off. A super cell, a thunderstorm that had spawned rotating clouds, was being shoved around by lateral winds. The rotating cloud pitched over and funneled into the southwestern part of the state and then plowed northeast, bearing down directly on Indianapolis. The front was expected in my neighborhood on the north side of town at 2:50 that afternoon, but the local TV weathermen had tracked the actual funnel cloud further south. The event was anticlimactic for us northsiders. A little ice, some wind, nothing big. The southern suburbs were another matter.

One tornado ripped through Southport, a suburban town just north of Greenwood, pulling the roof off of a sporting goods store and completely imploding a vacant Pier 1 Imports. A mother and child were picked up in their minivan, carried over a house, and deposited safely in a neighbor's yard. They emerged from the van without a scratch. A pregnant woman in the showers at the Baxter YMCA in Southport was pulled from her stall by an employee and dragged to the basement just three minutes before the cinderblock wall she'd been standing next to had collapsed along with much of the roof. The twister then turned due north, its path to youth hockey's beloved Perry Park abruptly altered. Perry was perhaps a quarter-mile from the Baxter Y.

The tornadoes had cut a swatch through the middle of Indiana that set meteorological records for the state. No twister had ever stayed on the ground as long as the one that screamed though the southern suburbs.

Even in January of 2003, nearly five months after the twisters, Southport and the northern edge of Greenwood still looked like a war zone. Blue tarps covered most of the YMCA and many of the simple brick ranch homes in the neighborhood. The Baxter's sign was a skeleton. The trees gave the most distinct and frightening gauge of the storm's strength and width. Fully branched maples and sycamores gave way suddenly to barren trunks whose limbs had been shortened by the wind and then the tree surgeons. This continued for perhaps the length of two football fields before the vegetation looked normal again.

Nobody in Greenwood suggested naming any of the local youth teams after twisters. People who have actually seen cyclones aren't too keen on being reminded of them.

A lot of the kids on Oliver's team that year lived within a few miles of Perry Park. They knew everybody in the joint, from the concessionaire to the kid who took your three bucks if you wanted to rent an ancient pair of skates. Some had seen their houses damaged by the winds that previous September. Some had roomed together when the power had gone out after the twisters struck. Amy and I were north-siders. The two sides of Indy couldn't be more different.

Indiana is bordered by Michigan above and Kentucky below. I-70 runs right through the middle of Indianapolis. I've often postulated that, like the Mason-Dixon Line, the Interstate is where the North ends and the South begins.

Amy and I pulled into Perry an hour ahead of game time. Some parents shot wary glances at one another. Some greeted each other warmly. My wife chatted with anyone who'd listen, and the more my Amy spoke, the more it looked to me like maybe a few of the Yanks and Rebs on the team were starting to lighten up.

The Indy Junior Ice won both games against Decatur. The next day, the Champaign Chiefs, looking evil in their black jerseys with the word CHIEFS emblazoned diagonally across the chest a la the New York Rangers, completely took our kids apart. The Ice were outskated and outshot for two back-to-back games, although our offspring gave everything they had for six brutal periods.

Every parent lined up as the kids walked off the bench and past the gauntlet of adults. A select group gave kids and coaches a hand when they left the rink and headed to the locker room. The applause was warm and genuine. A number of voices could be heard above the din: "Nice job! Good hustle! No quit on this team! Way to play! Good job, Coach! Way to stay after it. *You played a good game.*"

I had to smile. Amy and her like-minded counterparts—mainly women, mind you—had made the determination that whether you liked the coach or hated him, whether you thought that any other parent was a complete idiot or not, this was the team and the team deserved a hand. By complimenting child and coach alike—LOUDLY—maybe one camp could shame the other group into something that might approach tolerance.

It seemed to work.

The following weekend featured four games at Pan Am Plaza in Downtown Indy—two on Saturday, two on Sunday. (Like most hockey games at Ollie's level, the kids played three twelve-minute periods in rapid succession, followed by an hour's rest before the kids took the ice and did it all over again. Exhausting? Hell, it's exhausting just to watch.) The Saturday games against the Butler County Blackhawks from Oxford, Ohio, were brilliant. The kids were skating together, passing the puck, and remembering their positions.

Our wingers fed the puck to the center when the man was open; our centers knew to pass the puck off to the side when somebody else had a better shot. Skaters moved toward the opposing goaltender in tandem, one skating in to pass or shoot as the next skater set up for the rebound in case the goalie knocked the puck back into play. Our defensemen shot the puck from the blue lines and backed away in perfect anticipation of the play moving back in their direction. The kids bumped but didn't check; they used their sticks for shooting but not for tripping. They played with all the focused teamwork of a group of college-age kids ready to take on the Soviets in Lake Placid in 1980.

The Junior Ice lost both games by a single goal.

The parents held their emotions in check. With the exception of a single outburst—a mom yelling at her kid to go sit on the bench if he wasn't going to try—the adults simply applauded and cheered for good plays. As a group, we were no longer the Gambino crime family. We were, for now anyway, morphing into the Baileys from *It's a Wonderful Life*.

Sunday brought it home.

The Evansville Riverboat Gambling Addicts—alright, their real name was the Evansville Thunder—came into Pan Am for a pair that got underway at 8 a.m. This required leaving our house at seven o'clock, which required getting up at six o'clock on a black morning with a temperature of negative-two degrees Fahrenheit. Hockey weather.

The Indy Junior Ice blasted off the bench. The refs were

letting the kids hit this day. Our bigger guys (Oliver included) went right to work. The Junior Ice delivered a thumping to the Thunder—kids were pinned to the boards, and the defense rolled through and over smaller forwards while the offense seemed to find every open man in front of the net and actually get the puck to that person. We won, 6–2.

Breaking a losing streak has a curative effect. A big win can boost morale well beyond any playing field. The legendary NFL franchises from Pittsburgh and Dallas gave their fans respite from the collapse of the steel mills and the great oil busts. Joe Louis and Jackie Robinson gave hope to a vast nation of disenfranchised peoples. Laid off autoworkers have had their Red Wings and their Pistons offer them sweet diversion.

The Ice's scale was not nearly as grand, but that win helped to patch up the rift among the parents.

The next game was a lot tighter. Evansville's kids came out skating strong, finessing their way around our lumbering defenders. They went up 1–0 in the first minute.

The hits kept coming. The Indy Ice parents had abandoned the bleachers in Pan Am to crowd around the boards at the north end of the rink, just behind the net. A huge hit between Oliver and a kid from Evansville wearing number ninety-nine carried them both violently into the boards. Ninety-nine left Oliver with a parting punch. Amy, standing on the other side of the glass from the action, yelled, "Hey, now, little boy!" The other parents roared with laughter. Amy had invented the courteous heckle.

With the score tied 3–3 in the third period, the parents behind the net decided—spontaneously—to do the wave. In succession, every mom and dad, friend and foe alike, raised his or her arms and gave the tribal call of "*Gooooooo* Ice!" as the wave rippled falteringly along. It was goofy, it was stupid, and it was fun. I stood with Amy on my right, dads Pete and Randy on my left. Amy pestered me to explain the various whistles and hand signals, while Pete and Randy and I explained the blue and red line rules and praised one another's kids. Pete's son, you remember, was Jeremy, number eighty-eight on defense, a kid who complimented Oliver well in the other D position; Randy's boy was Cody, one of Oliver's best buds on the team and a tiny offensive speedster with little fear of a collision.

With less than a minute to go in the third, Ken's son Jared picked a pass away from the Thunder at roughly center ice. Seeing the coach's son, John Michael, ahead of him by fifteen feet and wide open, Jared slid the puck neatly toward his best friend on the team. The two had been playing together since they'd learned how to skate, and they ranked first and second on the team in total goals scored.

J.M. rolled across the blue line toward the Evansville goal. The Thunder's defense had time to readjust, putting a man on John and sending another toward Jared, who was crossing into the Evansville zone (the area between the blue line and the back boards, roughly a third of the rink) with Cody. John shot a pass to the open ice on his right. Jared grabbed the puck. The Evansville defender, pondering whether he should back up, whether he should cover Jared or cover Cody, got too aggressive. He rifled toward Jared, who faked the kid out of his skates, ducking right, then left around him. Jared shot the puck toward the net from a dozen feet away. The puck came in high above the goalie's outstretched glove and slid in just under the top pipe of the goal. This is called "puttin' one on the top shelf." The score was now 4–3 with twenty-five seconds remaining, and that's how it ended.

The Junior Ice went bananas. Gloves flew into the air. A whoop went up from the bench. Kids skated around with one knee up, moving their free arms in the classic starting-the-lawnmower-make-a-fist-and-pull victory gesture. It was the first time in three months that the Indy Junior Ice Squirt A team had won a one-goal game.

The kids lined up in the middle of the rink for one of the grandest traditions in sports. All the players on both teams lined up to skate past one another single file, shaking hands, tapping gloves, and exchanging the words "good game." This is a moment to make peace and extend the hand of good sportsmanship with every member of the opposing team, including that rotten little motherless bastard who tried to trip you on the way back to the bench during a time-out when the refs weren't looking.

It made me think—a lot—about what had happened to me over the course of the season. My head had come full circle. It hadn't been pleasant, but I felt like my attitude was returning to a state where my expectations were secondary to my son's.

Getting into the game was fine; getting angry was scary.

I had noticed that my intensity level had a very definite and very dark side effect. *I was getting pissed at my son when he made a mistake.*

There had been isolated instances when—and thank God I hadn't vocalized them too loudly—I'd been expecting to see a flawless game-day performance from my preadolescent offspring. I wanted him, by turns, to make the play, be the hero, do his best, all the things I've mentioned with various levels of shame—but I also wanted him to absolutely and completely avoid *screwing things up.*

I wanted to yell at him when a better skater blew past him. I wanted to chew him out for coming off the bench too slowly to relieve another player. I wanted to ground the poor little bugger for forgetting his position on a play. I wanted to scream at the kid—and not just "Oliver, think!" I wanted to insult and criticize. My brain was crossing the line from Involved Parent to Total A-hole. Could my mouth be far behind?

I knew my emotions were running hot. Hell, I was in the live broadcasting business—screw-ups were loud, public things that generated vicious reactions. My job wasn't surgery or manning an air-traffic screen at O'Hare, but there was pressure and performance anxiety just the same. At work, I had the ability to bitch quickly, bitch loudly, settle the issue and move on. I also had the ability to shut up about it. So far, I'd behaved myself at Oliver's hockey games, but the line between what I was cooking internally and what some other parents were saying aloud was getting a bit too thin.

Amy and I had raised our eyebrows at one another when some of the moms or dads had boiled over during a game. The drive home always featured a mumbling discussion of Those Who Behaved Badly right after Oliver started his inevitable in-the-car nap. A few parents seemed to think that a scout for the Michigan Wolverines or the Red Wings minor-league affiliate might pop into Indy to see a bunch of ten-year-olds play at any time. Now I was facing the demon myself. I had an interior monologue running that sounded a helluva lot like Those Who Behaved Badly.

I was coming back to the question that had been nagging me. *What do you expect?* Why are you upset at this little kid? Your little kid? If he knocks over a plant because he's running through the house with his hockey stick and *you told him not to I don't know how many times*, fine, you've got a right to yell, to punish. If your child is outplayed on a hockey rink by another child with more training or a God-given gift for speed on the frozen pond, you'd better sit back and admire that other child.

The debate would rage in my brain:

Your kid tanks the play. How in the hell does that affect you? Are you less of a dad? Less of a parent? Less of a man? What has he done to you by letting a forward get past him? He's been beaten by a kid whose entire childhood is disappearing in a string of locker rooms and stinking shoulderpads, a kid who doesn't climb trees or fly kites or ride his bike or play with his LEGOs because he's got to practice, practice, and practice hockey some more.

Is that little *wunderkind* playing hockey because he loves hockey? Or is he playing because Mom and Dad have invested all this time and all this money and heartache and hope and now— well, now it's just a job? Just a job. Something the kid has to do because it's expected, because it must be done, like homework or taking out the trash or feeding the dog.

Hey, maybe your boy was just outskated by a kid who was faster. Better. Ate more Wheaties that day. Got more sleep on Friday night. Didn't go swimming when he got to the hotel. What do you care? Suppose your kid blunders a long division problem on a test and drops his grade from a B to a C. Do you freak out? Do you scream? Do you ground him for a single mistake? Or do you try to help him learn so he'll nail it next time? Why the hell should a hockey game carry more weight than arithmetic?

It didn't. Seeing Ollie and his teammates wrap the game, tromp down to the locker room, and begin pulling off their gear, win or lose, there was always the same discussion, the same burning issue:

When are we going out for pizza?

The kids could drop a game by twenty goals or win by one. It didn't matter. There was always another game. The play-by-play continued to run inside their little skulls. They each would be a star at least once per match. Most of the kids wanted to play hockey so they could feel the singular moments: a great shot, a steal, a defensive play that stirred their parents into applause. They lived for those moments, not so much for the final score.

You lost, you won, who cared? You went home, you hung your equipment in the garage, you took a bath, you watched cartoons.

Yeah, some of the kids were uptight. Some of the kids would dwell on the final score. They'd be angry. They'd behave badly. Occasionally they'd get tossed from the game. They were, without exception, kids whose parents became vocal when their children made mistakes.

They weren't nearly as tragic as the kids whose talent became lost in their fear.

Two children on Ollie's team—kids with innate ability—always seemed to hold back. Amy had made the connection. She'd noted that the two kids whose parents were the Holiest of Holy Terrors—the loudest, angriest, bitchiest couples—well, their kids were *scared to death of screwing things up.*

They were tentative. They skated away from plays. They never shot; they passed quickly. When they couldn't pass, they'd panic. Their parents would yell. The fear intensified. The panic grew. Disaster was imminent—a bad pass, a cheap goal, a breakaway for the other side. And at the end of every miserable play, at the end of every gut-wrenching mistake followed by shrieks of parental disapproval, the finger of blame was always pointed in the same direction—squarely at the coach.

Intermission: THE COACHES

The Indy Junior Ice Squirt A Travel Hockey team had two primary coaches: Coach Mike (the one who liked to throw his hat) and Coach Mac. I'd gotten to know Coach Mike at a pro game in Fort Wayne. The kids were playing four games against the Fort Wayne River Rats, a Squirt 'A' travel team just like ours. A few select parents and most of the team had decided to take in a pro game that evening to see how them big fellas skated. The slate featured a minor league matchup between the Fort Wayne Komets and a team from Missouri. It wasn't enough to see four youth hockey games in thirty-six hours—hell, no! Let's go watch another hockey game!

The game was played in the Fort Wayne War Memorial, a venue that was undergoing a multi-million-dollar renovation. The kids were geeked. They had played two games that Saturday afternoon on the very same ice where the big guys were about to play.

Ollie and I got a ride to the rink with Randy and his boy Cody. Fort Wayne seemed to be the world leader in strip joints per capita. Between the hotel and the arena, we counted no less than four "Gentlemen's Clubs." There were so many that the town seemed to have run out of names for them. "Illusions 4" sat right across the street from "Temptresses II." Ollie and Cody threatened to jump out at every red light and "go look at boobies." It was tough not to encourage them.

We rolled up to the War Memorial. A bitter wind ripped the parking lot. Fort Wayne constantly took a pounding from the freshwater-fed snows off Lake Michigan. We were amazed at the size of the crowd on such a terrible night. The place was jammed.

We found our seats. Coach Mike had brought quite a few kids, as had Ken and his wife, Linda. The boys sat in a row together in the upper deck of the War Memorial. They hurled candy bar wrappers at each other and argued about which team they should root for.

"We're playin' against Fort Wayne all weekend! They're the *enemy*. I say Missouri."

"Fort Wayne is in Indiana, and so is Indianapolis, so you *gotta* root for Fort Wayne!"

Whenever someone scored, one half of the kids punched the other half in the shoulder.

The building was spectacular. Banners celebrating the long history of the venue hung in all four corners of the rink. The old NBA team, the Fort Wayne Pistons, was represented. So was Elvis and a male figure skater wearing leather pants. Coach Mike pointed up at the figure skater. "Didn't know they allowed that sort of thing in Fort Wayne," he laughed.

That was Coach Mike in a nutshell. Mike was generally quiet off the ice, but really enjoyed the kind of humor that bounced around the walls of a locker room. Laughing at a fart was thoroughly acceptable. Handing a thirsty kid a sport bottle from the portable rack and announcing, "Have a little toilet water!" was a classic Coach Mike punchline.

Coach Mac was less of a cutup. Mac had a Southern Hoosier accent. As I've mentioned, the interstate that cuts through the center of Indianapolis seems to divide north and south. Residents of Indiana who hail from north of I-70 carry a trace of the Great Lakes honk. South of Indy, the accent turns to a slow drawl that broadens as you approach the Ohio River and the part of the state known as Kentuckiana. (It's called Kentuckiana because, as I've heard many a comic say, that term sounds a hell of a lot better than "Indiucky.") Coach Mac sounded like he'd been born just north of Louisville.

"Y'all lost that gaime. Why?" Mac extended the last vowel in the word "why" so you almost heard an "a" in it. "'Cause y'all didn't play y'all's positions proper. Why? 'Cause y'all ain't been listenin' to myssef and Coach Mike." (The "a" crept into the word "Mike," too.)

Understand: Neither Oliver nor any of the other kids complained about Mac. His criticisms were always measured, and he never raised his voice off the ice. Sure, both coaches would shout commands to the players from the bench—even something as coarse as "Move your ass!"—and occasionally give the refs a plaintive "Aw, c'mon!" but off the ice, the coaches seemed to keep the volume low and the demeanor calm.

A little more than one month into the season, Coach Mac started picking up overtime at the shop where he worked. As his workweek became longer and longer, Mac had to skip games and practices to keep his employer happy. A series of other dads on the team began to show up on the bench to assist Coach Mike. Randy made an appearance, but some parents complained that Randy didn't have his coaching certificate. The team tried out some more pops. One dad jawed too much, another didn't jaw enough. No matter what combination of adults was manning the bench during a Junior Ice Squirt A Travel game, there was at least one parent in the group who was unhappy with the coaching lineup.

The grousing had originally begun back in December, when the team had voted for its captain and assistant captains.

In a private meeting between coaches and kids, Coach Mike had instructed the team to vote for one captain and two assistant captains. When the final results were tallied, the coach's son, John Michael, had won the right to wear the letter C on the upper left-hand corner of his jersey, while Jared and Ollie were awarded the A's.

Upon hearing the results, a few parents assumed that the coach had rigged the voting.

Mike had told the parents: "I just told the kids to vote for who they thought was best for the job—no matter if they were on offense or defense or the coach's kid or whatever …"

Mike's choice of words couldn't have been more inflammatory. Unfortunately for Mike, even though the phrase "no matter if they were on offense or defense or the coach's kid" hadn't been uttered when he'd actually been addressing the kids, a number of parents assumed that it had. Mike had simply used the phrase to attempt to point out that he'd been striving for an unbiased ballot when he relayed the story to the parents later.

Ollie told us that Coach Mike's instructions had been plain and simple. According to Oliver, Mike's exact words had been: "Write down your choice for one captain and two assistant captains! Pick somebody who you think is a good leader! It can be anybody at all on the team." Ollie made it clear that the coach hadn't mentioned John Michael or anyone else specifically during his talk with the team.

The parents who didn't like Mike naturally assumed the worst. It's an old joke in youth hockey that the "C" on a child's jersey doesn't mean "Captain," it stands for "Coach's Kid." Despite a few protests confirming Mike's innocence—even from some of their own kids—one camp of adults was certain that Mike had implied that a vote for John Michael was the politically expedient thing to do if a kid wanted ice time.

From what I knew of Mike, this couldn't have been possible. He only sat kids who weren't giving it all they had—and he was toughest on his own child.

As for my boy, Ollie thought Coach Mike was terrific. He appreciated his coach's humor and easygoing style with the team after a game. He could be stern when the kids weren't focused, but his voice after a loss was always reassuring. His attitude after a victory seemed equally restrained. A loss was something to learn from, but so was a win.

I had seen coaches, red-faced with rage, screaming at refs and children as young as six. I had seen coaches taken from the bench and escorted out of the rink. I had seen king-hell grade-A jerks who'd stumbled into a position of authority over fifteen or sixteen trembling preadolescent boys, men who expected small children to play like someone making a seven-figure income. I considered Ollie to be very, very lucky.

I couldn't figure why anyone with Mike's personality would volunteer to coach a youth team in any sport. Even though I hate them, the small-scale Hitlers and Napoleons who coach youth sports are easy to understand. They are obviously guys who need to compensate for the lack of control they feel over their own lives. They use coaching as a way to tell the world they are important. It is a pity that their reigns of terror usually come at the expense of a dozen or so terrified children, though. The only positive thing about a dictatorial youth sports coach is that he didn't decide to become a high school guidance counselor instead.

But why would a guy like Mike subject himself to the constant criticism he was bound to hear from some of the parents? There was sure to be at least one mom or dad affiliated with a team at this level who felt that the only thing keeping his or her little Lemieux out of the NHL was Mike's decision to start the kid on defense instead of center. I knew for a fact that some of the parents questioned Mike's decisions so often that their kids had simply stopped listening to their own coach. If Coach tells you to pass, but Mom says you should try and break for the net, whom should you listen to? For a ten-year-old, the choice is simple: *Obey the one who feeds me.*

I felt terrible for Mike every time a parent chewed him out. During one practice, a hockey mom decided to have a pretty animated chat with Mike regarding her boy's ice time. As Mike turned his attention from the drills he'd been running to try and reason with someone who was obviously upset, I noticed something amazing. The kids were running the drills by themselves.

As soon as they noticed the coach wasn't paying attention, the kids had two obvious choices: goof off or keep working. The captain and his assistants shouted instructions, and the kids moved from drill to drill, shooting, skating, sprinting from line to line, passing, skating forward and then backward around the circles—the children knew the drills and the order in which to run them. The coach had done his job. These kids wanted to work for him, no matter what.

But Mike couldn't enjoy it. He had his cap low over his eyes, hands jammed in his pockets. He was trying to calm an angry mother.

I had an inclination of what Mike was dealing with. I'd had a taste myself.

I had assisted the head coach of Ollie's soccer team during the one and only summer that Ollie had played the sport. Oliver had played in a YMCA league in Indy, and I was recruited to stand by the goalie and warn him that the play was coming his way. The Y league was pretty informal—more about recreation than competition—and the kids rotated through each position on the field as they learned the fundamentals of the game. As a result, the goalie coach found himself talking to a series of kids who had no interest in tending goal whatsoever.

In fact, for most of the Y kids, the whole idea of playing a soccer game ranked behind "talking to my friends from school" and "running from yellowjackets" on the "List of Things to Do *During* a Soccer Game." I vividly remember yelling, "Heads up! Here comes a scorer on a fast break!" and realizing I was yelling to an empty net. My tender had wandered clear off the field behind the goal, sat down, and begun trying to fish a pebble out of one of his cleats.

The other team scored. The goalie's mom began yelling epithets at me that could've taken the "Christian" right out of "Young Men's Christian Association."

When the Fort Wayne Komets and the Missouri Mississippi River Flood Victims (alright, I made that one up, too) were pounding the crap out of each other, I got the chance to ask Coach Mike why he coached.

"I get to spend a lot of time with John Michael," was his answer.

It was more than that. He liked to teach. He liked kids. He loved hockey. But the party line never wavered: Mike coached in order to *spend more time with the family.*

JANUARY—3rd PERIOD

On Super Bowl Sunday, the Indy Junior Ice was scheduled to play an early morning doubleheader against the Squirt All-Stars, a level lower than travel.

Time-Out: LEVELS

Before we get back to the season at hand, a word of explanation as to how the skill levels are divided in youth hockey. Here's how the levels break down specifically:

House teams are made up of entry-level kids. A particular rink fields a number of teams that play one another just at that rink alone. The various teams are usually named after big-league pro squads and often carry huge company logos on their jerseys. Sponsors can get their names plastered all over house-league jerseys, which makes for some pretty interesting combinations. Ever seen a matchup between the J & D Trucking Penguins and Bob's Landscaping Wild?

All-Stars (or **Select** teams) are the best kids culled from a rink's house teams. Teammates on the All-Stars play each other during House games. They do some limited traveling.

Travel teams are made up of kids who are too advanced for the House leagues. Larger towns field more than one travel team in a particular age bracket. Oliver's team was an "A" level, which was, again, a level below the "AA" Travel Squirts.

RESUME PLAY

The first game started at 7:15 Sunday morning. About half the team had spent Friday night at Cody's house for a birthday sleepover. They'd violated the curfew the coach would've imposed at any hotel: They'd stayed up until 5 a.m., woke up at 9, and still hadn't recouped a proper amount of rest by the time Sunday morning rolled around. A number of kids were fighting the flu, and a surprise snowstorm had made the drive to Pan Am plaza pretty dicey, so more than a few had opted to stay home. The travel team was under-manned and skating slowly, and only bested the All-Stars by a score of 4–2.

The second game was brutal. The scoreboard had stopped counting travel goals at ten, but every kid in the rink knew what the score really was at any given time during the game.

With half of the third period gone and the game all but won, Coach Mike put Oliver at right wing—on offense. At first, Ollie seemed out-of-sorts with the whole notion of skating forward—defensemen were usually traveling backward throughout the game. Ollie fed the puck toward the middle when his team moved into his opponent's zone and began to get the feel of the position. With five minutes to go in the game, Ollie finally got the shot he'd been waiting for all year.

After charging a loose puck on the enemy goalie's right and nudging a defender out of position, Ollie backed toward the net as he glanced over his left shoulder. Ollie faked a move forward, then flipped the puck backhand toward the net. The puck hit a defender's shinpad, then caromed off the goalie's right skate and dribbled across the goal line for a slow-speed point.

Oliver led the defensemen on his team in assists, but the shooting gods had been kind only to the forwards all season. Ollie had fired innumerable pucks at the net from just inside the blue line, but hadn't seen one go in without a pop from a teammate. After three months of travel hockey, Ollie had finally managed to put one in by himself. He raised his stick in victory, free arm pumping, one leg up. Ollie scored the goal that brought the actual score up to 19-2. The travel team would put in two more by the end of the game, including one from Freddy, another big defender.

A few of the All-Star parents grumbled about the wide margin of victory. Others realized that with the game completely over by the start of the third period, Coach Mike had begun moving players out of their usual positions. As the teams tromped along the rubber floor on the outside of the boards and headed toward the locker room, a parent from the All-Star team tapped me on the shoulder. He was an older gent, dressed all in black with a black cowboy hat. He looked like a graying Jerry Glanville, the old NFL Falcons coach.

"Y'all travel fellers play position that well ev'ry game?" he inquired.

"Usually," I said, "but today they were exceptional."

The cowpoke nodded. "That's a well-coached team, yer travel fellers."

I smiled at Glanville. "I'll pass that along," I said.

Time-Out: THE CELEBRATION OF THE SCORE

When I was a tyke playing Pop Warner football, my coach, Des Burns, a man who chain-smoked through practice and—though none of us knew it—was dying from massive liver failure, always admonished us: "When you get into the end zone, don't overdo it. Act like you've been there before."

The fundamental problem with such sage advice? There's always at least one time when you *haven't* been there before.

Once, during a game I wasn't able to attend, Oliver managed to carry the puck from behind his own net, skate it clear down the ice, and fire it in for an unassisted point. When I got the chance to talk to him about it, he described it thusly:

"I scored and then skated all the way around the rink in front of the other team's fans and looked every one of them *right in the eye.*"

Okay—was the goal low or high? Did you deke or juke or just plain shoot it where the goalie wasn't? Did the goalie drop while you shot high? Did you shoot from the left or the right? Were you close to the goal or just across the blue line?

"Close up, glove side, just above his hand. But I looked at every one of their fans *right in the eye.*"

At a practice at Pan Am, I asked our team manager, Ken, when—and why—his son Jared had begun to play. Like me, Ken could barely skate, and he told me that Jared had been watching the Mighty Ducks movies when ... (KILL EMILIO KILL EMILIO KILL EMILIO) ...when he'd asked his Dad if he could try hockey. Jared's dad had rented gear for the first few months until he realized that Jared had a very natural ability. The game came easy to him. Ken told me the kid had learned to skate in about ninety minutes, and had immediately demonstrated an innate understanding of how a hockey game flowed.

Jared had it nailed, and a kid who understands the beauty of a game like hockey at such a tender age will always carry a fondness for the sport. A kid who understands hockey early knows it's about flying faster than a runner can run, weaving through traffic to shoot and score and celebrate like mad.

Jared hadn't nailed the whole celebration ritual, though. According to Ken: "I'll never forget the first time he scored. I was watchin' through the glass in the lobby at Perry Park when he put one in the net. He went for the bench and left the rink, then he came out to the lobby to give me a high-five. Game was still goin' on, of course."

Jared had since learned to stay on the ice after a successful wrist shot. Jared and his teammates had learned a lot—and grown a lot since they'd been Mini-Mites. During the season Jared and Oliver played Squirt together, Jared and the rest of his teammates seemed to outgrow their putrid equipment weekly. At every practice, somebody would show up with new pants or shin guards or—smile, Hockey Dads, this might just be a reference to the heir to *your* estate—cup. By late January, our precious bundles of joy had morphed into giant stinking, snarling monsters with bloodlust in their eyes.

 **Intermission:** THE RENAISSANCE KID

Alright, so the child wasn't eating raw meat for breakfast, lunch, and dinner. He was growing rapidly, though, and on occasion he looked as if his basic motor skills would never catch up to the extra length being added to his arms and legs every day. His mom, convinced the boy needed to be as graceful, mannerly, and well rounded as possible, signed him up for a twice-a-month Indianapolis institution: Mrs. Kinnear's Cotillion.

Mrs. Kinnear, I'd been told, was the mother of the actor Greg Kinnear. This seemed to make sense: Greg was from a town in Indiana called Logansport, and perhaps, I figured, he'd even sent ol' Mom enough coin to keep the Cotillion afloat during the occasional Cotillion recession. As it turned out, this information was incorrect. Mrs. Kinnear had a son, but he was named Kenneth. Kenneth Kinnear had never hosted a clip show on the E! network or shown up in a Jack Nicholson movie.

Kenneth Kinnear's mom was also somewhat older than Greg Kinnear's mom. Kenneth Kinnear's mom had been teaching kids how to be Young Gentlemen and Ladies for approximately six thousand years. Adults who attended the woman's Cotillions back in their youth seemed to remember Mrs. Kinnear as being an old woman back then.

A cotillion, for those who aren't familiar with the concept, is a ballroom dance complete with a receiving line and the prerequisite punch and cookies. (It's also a lot more popular in Dixie than in the rust belt country where hockey is most popular.) The boys were expected to wear jackets and ties, and the girls wore shiny shoes and white gloves. Mrs. Kinnear taught them the steps: foxtrot, waltz, some uncomplicated swing moves. Mrs. Kinnear stood at the center of the room, announcing changes in partners and steps as her husband played piano and an incredibly bored drummer brushed the top of a snare. The children learned protocol—how to introduce and be introduced, how to fetch punch and cookies, how to shake hands and stand up straight. (Oliver commented that cotillion was "the easiest thing in the world for a girl. She just *sits* there while you bring her food and stuff.") I got all of this information secondhand—Oliver's mom had been taking the boy to cotillion against my better judgement.

"Good Lord," I told her, "sounds like punching bag lessons."

"What do you mean?" Amy demanded.

"Oh, c'mon. If any of his hockey buds finds out he's been putting on a tie once a week to go waltz with the nerd brigade, he's going to spend most of this season getting his butt kicked."

Amy glowered. "A bunch of the kids from the team are there, too."

Amy wanted Oliver to be a gentleman. She was, I'm sure, also secretly mortified by my style of dance: move arms at right angles to body, shuffle feet, bite lower lip like you're doing a chipmunk impression. Maybe she saw a glimmer of hope for our boy's steppin' abilities if she could only intervene early in his development. Apparently it wasn't enough that the kid could skate backward and his old man could barely set blade on the ice without looking like a drunk on a boat in a hurricane.

Amy took Oliver to Mrs. Kinnear's Cotillion every other week throughout the winter. I didn't protest, but I didn't get involved, either. I took the kid to the Indy 500 and NASCAR races while Mom stayed home, so this was something she could handle without me.

Until the final dance arrived.

Ever the involved parent, Amy had a meeting at Oliver's school on the very same night he was to attend the final cotillion of the season. "You don't have to stay," Amy told me. "Just drop him off and pick him up. And make sure he wears a clean shirt and a nice tie."

I made sure the boy was ready, checked his shirt, tied his tie, and lent him some dark socks—all he seemed to own were the thick white or gray variety made for the inside of a pair of hockey skates. The child also borrowed some of my cologne—okay, he borrowed half the bottle. It's easy for a kid to get carried away with the smelly stuff.

I drove the boy to Mrs. Kinnear's Cotillion and dropped him off. He didn't want me to come in. He didn't even want me to get out of the car. He dashed into an office building and disappeared down the stairs to the basement room where the cotillion was held. Other kids were trickling into the building as I drove away.

I spent an hour buying groceries—well, actually, I spent forty-five minutes browsing the snack aisle and fifteen minutes buying food with actual nutritional value. (You can always tell who has gone to the market last by the ratio of chips to produce in our pantry.) When I returned to Mrs. Kinnear's, the cotillion was still in full swing.

I took the stairs down to the cellar and peered through the glass door into the cotillion room. Roughly a hundred kids were in the room, fifty of them paired up boy/girl and dancing together, the balance sitting on folding chairs. A group of parents sat along one wall, dressed to the nines and observing everything that was happening on the dance floor. The term that leapt to my head was "practice prom." Mrs. Kinnear stood in the middle of the floor, calling steps and directing her assistant, a middle-aged woman in a black dress, to tap the shoulders of various couples who—wait a second. This was a dance contest!

My son was waltzing with a pale blonde girl who was perhaps two inches taller than him. She was smiling. Oliver was grinning at his buds as he moved across the floor, and a few of his teammates who'd already been disqualified gave him the thumbs up. Several of the girls who'd been relegated to the sidelines waved and yelled congratulations at Ollie and the blonde girl.

"Oliver! Katie! You guys are great! Oliver! Oliver!"

Half the little girls knew my kid's name—and seemed to be vying for his attention. I was dumbfounded. I wasn't raising Bobby Orr. I was raising James Bond.

Mrs. Kinnear's helper noticed one boy tromping all over the feet of his dance partner. She tapped the couple on the shoulder.

"You may sit down now, please."

The boy's dance partner, a delicate child in a flowered dress, punched the guy in the middle of his chest. The kid staggered backward and dropped onto his keister as the girl he was dancing with stamped off to the spectators' seats.

More kids were asked to leave the floor. Mrs. Kinnear and her helper thinned the field to five couples—including my son and the girl named Katie.

My boy—my boy who thought that the musical world began with Green Day and ended with System of a Down—my boy was dancing to The Greatest Hits of the 1940s. He was also doing a damn fine job.

The call went out for a foxtrot, then a waltz, then three or four steps whose names I did not recognize. Mrs. Kinnear pointed to a couple thirty feet away from her. "First!" she called.

She pointed at Katie and Oliver. "Second!"

Now I was truly awestruck. Second place. The little thug who couldn't wait to graduate into a hockey league that allowed him to skate full speed at another child while wielding a stick had just placed second in a ballroom dancing contest—and his buds were congratulating him.

Oliver and Katie posed for pictures. They bid farewell to their friends and then one another. Oliver and I went to the car, and my boy pondered the trophy that he'd just been handed.

"I felt kinda bad for Katie that we didn't come in first."

I glanced at the boy, still wearing his tie and jacket underneath the winter coat with the Junior Ice logo emblazoned on the chest.

"She didn't seem to mind," I said.

"Oh, yeah—second out of, like, fifty couples was pretty good."

Indeed.

His mom was excited when she heard the news. "And what did Mrs. Kinnear say to you when you won?" she asked Oliver.

Oliver pondered the question. "Not much. I think she was trying to remember my name. She asked me like three times. She's kind of old, Mom."

Mrs. Kinnear had handed the kid and his partner each a trophy, though—a small cup perched on a marble base. And now, sitting on his room on a shelf amongst the figures of hockey players, sticks down and bent forward, perched above plaques that read "Mite" and "Squirt" and "Travel," "MVP" and "League Champions," there's a small trophy bearing a plaque that reads:

MRS. KINNEAR'S COTILLION—2ND PLACE

Our precious little hockey-playin', punk-rock playin', rough and tumble bundle of joy was also a smooth-dancin' stud.

Go figure.

J

FEBRUARY—1ˢᵗ PERIOD

By early February, our precious little bundles of joy had also learned how to scare the bejesus out of their moms and dads.

So much for ballroom dancing: The kids had learned how to send a puck in high and fast against the Plexiglas above the boards. This made a pleasing sound—especially if you managed to pop the stainless steel and aluminum brackets that framed the glass. Hitting the glass made a terrifically loud *thunk*, but ringing one off the frame rivaled the report from a mid-caliber handgun.

The game was simple: Rap a puck off the glass as close as you could to the target provided by the adult face on the other side. Extra credit if that face belonged to one of your parents. Make Mom yelp, and you were kickin' ass. Make Dad wince, and you'd achieved the pinnacle of cool. When they were lining up to drill in the curved corners of the rink, the kids would send a flurry of rubber biscuits into the glass. Adults would grunt and snap their heads away, trying not to look as if their little fifth-grader had just spiked their blood pressure with a ripping slap shot at the spectators. Show no weakness, Father! Give no quarter, Mother!

At the slightest sign of fear, the little buggers might just attack.

Attack, indeed. The little buggers could have outfought us easily if they'd put their minds to it. Dressed in their feudal warlord gear and wielding sticks, the Indy Junior Ice could've overrun adult society and installed their own government. The little buggers were tough and well padded.

Attack, indeed. The little buggers weren't little at all. By Martin Luther King Jr. Day, Oliver was outgrowing his hockey pants to the point where he was chafing underneath. Ollie outgrew pads and skates and socks—and then, one, day, we discovered he was outgrowing the family car.

The hockey and garment bag, the sticks and various other gear, the water bottles, the cooler, and the thermal blanket for the really cold rinks consumed the entire cargo area of our compact station wagon. Additionally, Ollie had taken an interest in playing the bass—the stand-up, acoustic, string double bass. Our week went as follows: Saturday, hockey games; Sunday, hockey games; Monday, bass practice; Tuesday, hockey practice; Wednesday, hockey practice. Thursday usually saw a school or work function demanding our time (Cotillion, anyone?), and Friday was a futile attempt at catching up on laundry.

The hockey crap was too big for the car. The double bass was too big for the car. My ten-year-old had outgrown an eighteen-thousand-dollar automobile.

Why, Lord, why couldn't Ollie have picked soccer and the clarinet? Handball and the violin? The piccolo and track? Some kind of sport and instrument combination that didn't require biweekly trips to the chiropractor on my part? I imagined a world in which all of Ollie's extracurricular activities fit into a tiny corner of the trunk, saving us all of that room and cash we'd blown on pads and bass rental. I imagined filling that space with gourmet food and craft beers—but hockey season dictated otherwise. We were too cramped and too broke. Ahh, SpaghettiOs and Bud ...

On the other hand, who the hell had time to actually heat up a can of Chef Boyardee anything? Hockey, bass, and the school play all precluded the idea of a sit-down meal. Microwave pizza was a struggle. I found myself eating larger and larger lunches so I wouldn't keel over with hunger by the time hockey practice wrapped on a Wednesday. Which brings me to ...

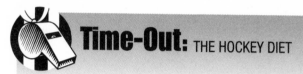

Time-Out: THE HOCKEY DIET

Pan Am Plaza had its own concession stand, but the damn thing never seemed to be open when anyone was hungry. The folks at Pan Am had a terrible time staffing the joint, and when they could find a semi-conscious teenager to man the counter, the kid always seemed to commit some pretty egregious culinary errors. One could expect a gastronomic experience that included the unique flavors of the Nacho Donut and the Coffee Dog.

As a result, a lot of parents wound up pumping quarters into the giant vending machines that sat in the basement of Pan Am. The machines were packed with some of the greatest junk food that American society has ever concocted. Combos and Fritos and Chex Mix—oh my! Cool Ranch Doritos! Andy Capp's Hot Fries! The fluffy salted Styrofoam packing material called Funyuns! A glance at the nutrition information on any package tells the story: four thousand ingredients that add up to 57 percent of the recommended daily allowance of sodium. I ate this crap on a regular basis. I was convinced my blood pressure was high enough to launch a rocket to the moon.

You can tell what is really horrible for you by simply checking the name of the product. There has never been a vegetable with the word "fun" in it, so Funyuns probably aren't bursting with vitamins. Skate-punk adjectives are another big tip: Anything calling itself "Extreme!" means "extra salt." If the word is spelled "X-Treme," you are looking at extra-extra salt and colors never, ever found in nature. "Bold" and "zesty" also indicate that you are buying a yummy sack of hypertension.

Here I was, week after week, watching my son and the rest of the Indy Junior Ice Squirt A Travel team condition themselves into young men and women with power and endurance while I shoveled salted fat into my face on the sidelines. Oliver and his teammates were growing up while three-quarters of the adults seemed to be growing out. How in the hell were we supposed to keep these kids in line? In order to punish 'em, we'd have to catch 'em first.

Our race of adult masters was doomed. Our kind would soon be obsolete. The kids were molding themselves into stick-waving, puck-slapping athletes, and we were sitting in the bleachers eating X-Treme Zesty Bold Nacho Donuts.

FEBRUARY—2nd PERIOD

On the first weekend of the month, I was shoveling two inches of heavy, wet snow from the driveway of our house. It was a Saturday, and Oliver had a pair of hockey games, the first scheduled to begin at noon. Amy opened the front door and called out to me. "Something's happened to the shuttle," she said. I was finishing my work, so it was just a few moments before I was able to shake the snow from my boots and step inside.

I watched the news with my wife on CNN. The space shuttle *Columbia*, traveling at twelve thousand miles per hour, had broken up as it tried to maneuver through the upper layers of Earth's atmosphere. Seven astronauts had been aboard. The ship was a total loss.

Every television set in the house was on and every radio was being monitored while I got ready to take Oliver to his games. All the video footage was equally unspectacular—a small bright point of light that split apart like inexpensive fireworks, drifting into small lines of smoke that could've been mistaken for the contrails of three or four jets flying in formation. I shaved and dressed.

The television replayed the image constantly. I was getting ready to take my son to a hockey game. Everything was normal on this Saturday morning except for that image on the television—a small shattering of light that represented the absolute destruction of seven human beings.

I loaded the car with Oliver's gear. We drove south through Indianapolis on Capitol Avenue. I was listening to a radio station that had a channel open for the official word from NASA's mission control center in Houston, and the local announcers would yield when the man in Texas began speaking. "This is Mission Control Houston …" began the voice with each message. The voice was strange, detached, and emotionless. He used words like "contingency" and "nominal," like a scientist detailing the flaws of a failed experiment. The only indication that a human disaster had occurred was the ominous warning about debris on the ground in Texas. Whatever had fallen to Earth might still be contaminated with rocket fuel, highly toxic propellants that could kill you if you inhaled the brown fog generated by the smoldering wreckage.

Oliver and I were silent as we listened to the radio. The announcer ended his report and then went to a break. The first commercial began with a jingle pitching carpet. Oliver and I gazed through the windshield as I drove.

The sun was struggling to beat through a hazy, thinly overcast sky. The city had a soft, silvery-gray, almost mother-of-pearl hue to it. The trees on the shoreline shimmered with a cover of melting snow as we crossed over Fall Creek on the old bridge. We could see downtown Indy just ahead: the twin antennae on the top of the Bank One building, the big hotels, and the RCA Dome. We drove through the good neighborhoods and the poorer section, by the hospitals and the factory where Stutz automobiles had once been manufactured.

The commercial break ended. The voice from Mission Control returned. NASA had declared a "contingency."

Seven families had lost a mother or a dad.

I was driving my son to a hockey game.

I had the strange feeling that Oliver and I had taken some kind of intermission from reality. We were going about the standard weekend rituals—pack the car, fill the water bottles, tape the sticks—while pieces of *Columbia* were still dropping into the Texas woodlands.

Which was normal? Which part made any sense? Why were we trudging through the day while every radio and television broadcast told us we should be grieving? Surely we shouldn't stop living. People died every day. The simple fact that my son and I were driving to a sporting event seemed somehow disrespectful, but I didn't see how we could've made any other choice.

The mood at the rink was dark. Most parents—and kids—had heard about the shuttle, and word spread quickly to those who hadn't. A TV in the pro shop at Pan Am Plaza was tuned to CNN, and those folks who weren't watching their children play hockey were crowded around the set. *Columbia* had been lost—and it was just another jab at a population swimming in bad news.

The attacks of September 11 were a recent memory then, only eighteen months old. War with Iraq looked certain, and the government of North Korea had restarted its nuclear programs. United Airlines was in financial trouble—layoffs were rumored to be imminent at the Indy maintenance center. Conseco, the big insurance firm up in Carmel, Indiana, was in bankruptcy. The state itself was going broke.

It didn't matter. All of it could wait. Our sons and daughters wanted to play hockey this day, and we wanted to watch them.

The Indy Ice Squirt A Travel team trudged into the locker

room. Jared had begun to complain of aches and chills, and John Michael said he was just getting over the flu. Cody had stayed home stick. Half the kids looked pale and tired. The team's record overall record stood at twenty-three wins, fifteen losses, and three deadlocks. The league record was another matter.

In league play—the Squirt A Buckeye league, the record that determined seeding for the championship tournament and the state competitions—the team was next to last with two wins, five losses, and one tie. Four of the five losses had been dropped by a single goal. That Saturday afternoon, Ollie's comrades faced a pair of league games against the Cincinnati Cyclones.

The first game was thirty seconds old when the parents in attendance stopped hating the world and started hating each other. Oliver dropped back in front of the goal as Cincy won the opening face off. The Cyclones' center went streaking toward net and shot. Matt, the goalie, covered the puck, but the center kept coming as the whistle blew.

Oliver's coaching kicked in. It was his job as a defenseman to protect his goalie, especially if the goalie lay prone and vulnerable. The center from Cincy rapped his stick into Matt's gloved hand and helmet, and Oliver, on top of all this action, responded by giving the kid from the Queen City a tremendous, violent shove, pushing his stick into his opponent crosswise.

The ref called Oliver for a two-minute bench minor penalty.

A parent from Cincy yelled over the boards: "YEAH, THAT'S THE WAY THESE LITTLE BASTARDS ALWAYS PLAY!"

A chorus of angry catcalls rang back. From Danny's father: "It's hockey, not figure skating, you bum!" From Zack's mom: "Why doncha sign yer kid up for ballet lessons!"

Two minutes later, the Cincy center who Oliver had fouled checked John Michael into the boards from behind. John Michael crumpled to the ice and didn't move for ten or fifteen frightening seconds. A bearded and stocky Cincy parent shouted, "Oh, you can dish it out but you can't take it!"

Coach Mike left the bench to check on his son, lying there on ice, twitching and stirring slowly. The Indy parents yelled back to the Cincy side across the rink, accusing the Cyclones of being cheap-shot artists. Coach Mike reached John Michael as the bearded man yelled, "Get up, you little baby!" Coach Mike, helping his boy to his feet, looked up and locked eyes with the bearded man. He said not a word, but the look spoke volumes: *Tough enough to heckle a ten-year-old, are you? Are you tough enough to go eyeball to eyeball with me?*

I smiled. Coach Mike wasn't about to start a fight, but he certainly looked as if he had the ability to end one. The look defused the situation. The parents still catcalled back and forth, but nobody wanted to see the thing degenerate into an actual physical confrontation. Had Mike shamed them or scared them? It didn't matter. He didn't need to say anything. The glare was enough.

Bob, Zack's old man, was standing next to me at one end of the rink. "Looks like we've got a rivalry cookin' with these Cincy guys," he remarked.

Ollie had told me that the Indy teams didn't have a rivalry with Cincy. The Indy teams had a rivalry with everybody. Ollie claimed that word was circulating through the Buckeye league that his team had a reputation as a gang of criminals, the Oakland Raiders of youth hockey. When I'd first heard that news, I'd shrugged it off as a preadolescent machismo. Now I wasn't so sure.

Was Indy getting a rap as the bully of the league? The parents from Cincinnati seemed to think that our kids were violent punks. I couldn't understand it. Ollie's penalties were usually the result of his attempts to track down a puck after the man holding the biscuit had already passed it—the kid was still learning how to time things. Oliver wasn't the enforcer ... the "cement head" ... the team goon ...

Was he?

The Junior Ice dropped game one to the Cyclones by a final of 4–2. The next game started an hour later, and I took my familiar place along the boards to the left and behind the net on the north end of the rink.

The Junior Ice Mite travel squad had just wrapped up a two-game stand against Dayton. The coaches of the Mite team wandered back into the rink to check out the Squirts. Oliver had played with a good number of the kids on this Mite team the previous year, but had graduated to Squirts while the younger ones remained behind. I knew both parents and coaches on this Mite team.

Matthew, the team's manager, and a couple of coaches named Karl and Danny sidled up beside me. Karl had played professional hockey, including a stint with the NHL's Chicago Blackhawks. "Okay," said Karl after his perfunctory hellos and small talk, "where's Oliver?"

I pointed to number seventy-four. "Big defender working the center in front of the goal," I replied.

Ollie and the Cyclone were tangled up. Oliver's job was to keep the center from getting a clean shot. He bumped and shoved the other kid, harassing his opponent just the way he'd been taught.

Karl and Danny began a patter with Matt that sounded like a Greek chorus calling the action in a mythic comedy.

"That ain't over, that one—he tripped him. There! Got him with his stick like he was startin' the lawnmower."

"Taylor's gonna smack him back, I know it. Pop! Got him!"

"Ollie's got him in the boards! Pin him! Thatta boy! Grind

him down! You'll be checking next year!"

"The only thing that would make this game better would be a cold barley sandwich."

"Or two."

"Or the seven you had last night."

"That wasn't beer. That was some light crap."

"Still had you singin' karaoke. HIT HIM, CHRISTIAN! LET 'IM KNOW YOU'RE ON 'IM!

The chatter continued. The morning's events were all but forgotten. The *Columbia* had momentarily, thankfully, faded ever so slightly in my memory.

Karl turned to me. "Ollie gets to play Pee Wee next year?"

"Yep," I said, "he can't wait to start checking."

Karl nodded. "He's big; he's tough. Pee Wee needs kids with size that can hit. Too many finesse players right now, I think. Need more tough guys."

Great. My sweet, sensitive, artistic, and thoughtful child was the Biker of the Boards, the Wrecker of the Rink. Some kids had tempers; my kid had bulk. It didn't matter how he reacted—he was big and he knew how to administer contact, ergo, he was the Honorary Goon of the Indy Junior Ice Squirt A Travel squad.

The upside? Ollie had the proper technique for anger management working in his favor. If a kid popped you in the facemask, you stared and waited for the ref to haul the other guy to the box. Returning the favor only meant you were headed to the penalty box as well, blowing the chance for your guys to play with a one-man advantage.

If you did get a penalty, you skated to the box, waited for the parent manning the box to open the door for you, and then sat down. End of activity for player.

Pete was working the door of the box that Saturday afternoon and wound up in the unfortunate position of having the two most demonstrative kids in the cube with him at the same time. Zack and John Michael had both been sent to the cell for a scuffle at the Cyclones' goal, and both immediately began banging their sticks around inside the box. Pete jumped up to stand on the bench, then suspended himself from the top of the glass to keep from having his kneecaps shattered. Wood and spit were flying constantly during the entire two minutes of the Ice's double penalty. The defense held Cincy in check, and every parent in the joint applauded our three-versus-five penalty kill (no points scored during a "power play," that is).

Down by a single goal at the start of the third, the Indy Junior Ice came off the bench at ripping speed. Ollie was dead in front of the net as a Cyclone swept across the Ice at an oblique angle to the goal. He was setting something up, maybe a shot or a pass to another player circling away from the boards. Ollie charged the puck handler aggressively. The kid never saw Oliver coming. The Cyclone turned his back as Ollie arrived, a moment too late for Oliver to stop. Ollie hammered through the kid from behind, and the ref blew his whistle immediately.

The Cincy parents let Oliver have it. A torrent of verbal abuse poured from the bleachers and into the penalty box. Oliver had never been called a punk-ass delinquent thug, had never been accused of parole violations, and had never heard anyone question the species of his birth parents. The kid sat and took the abuse.

The Cyclones scored with Ollie in the box. The game ended with Cincinnati up 4-2.

The teams filed past each other, shaking hands in the middle of the rink, and then went bounding down the rubberized stairs of Pan Am Plaza to their locker rooms. After the coaches had given the Ice their post-game assessment, I walked in to the Ice's haven to find Ollie half undressed and cradling his head in his hands. The kid was crying, very, very quietly, but crying nonetheless.

"What's wrong?" I asked.

"I didn't mean to hit that kid. I could've hurt him really badly," whispered Oliver.

"You didn't, though. He's fine."

"I let my team down," Ollie continued. "They scored when I was in the box."

"And they scored the other three when somebody else was in the box. Did the coach yell at you?"

Ollie shook his head. I was hunkered down in front of him. I got in close with my back to the room so no one could see us. I pulled out my handkerchief and wiped his eyes. "Everything's cool," I said. "I know you didn't mean to hit that kid, and so does everybody else on the team."

Ollie looked at me. "Okay," he said falteringly.

"You'll be fine. Try and pull it together at least until we get to the car." The kid could bawl all he wanted to when we got out of Pan Am. I knew he and I both would've hated for his teammates to see him crying right now.

I looked into Oliver's eyes. Amazing. The kid was worried about everybody but himself.

Amazing. I felt absolutely no anger whatsoever at the idiot parents who had heckled Oliver. What was I going to do? Kick in Cincy's locker room door and challenge the first parent I saw to a brawl? Lay in wait in the hallway and punch a Cyclone hockey dad for being stupid, for being ignorant, for heckling a ten-year-old and making the kid cry?

But Oliver didn't seem to give a damn about what he'd heard from the stands. He was worried about letting the team down or, worse, hurting somebody. Hearing somebody's old man yelling like a moron was a huge part of the game of hockey, even at this tender level. The players knew they'd hear it from the stands. They knew they were in for it the second they laced up the skates and strapped on the helmets. A blindside back check, though—nobody expected that, and nobody deserved it, even if it was a mistake.

Ollie stood up now, dry-eyed and smiling a little. I smiled back at him. He hadn't meant to clobber that kid, but it couldn't have been helped. The play had been solid; the timing had been poor. Ollie had committed to charging the guy too quick. It was a mistake he was bound to make at least once and probably more. He was learning.

He was growing up, too. The kid carried an honest-to-God manifestation of one of the biggest clichés in sport. The kid had heart—a lot of heart. Heart. What did that mean? Guts? Determination? Sportsmanship? Empathy? Compassion? All of it, I think. All of it.

I took my kid to a hockey game on a Saturday. He played his best at the game he loved. He thought he might've hurt someone, he thought he'd let the team down, but he hadn't.

Seven astronauts went down into Texas. They were an abstraction to me—a picture of seven people I'd never met being broadcast on CNN. It was terrible, it was tragic, but my son and I went to a hockey game on a Saturday. Life went on for the rest of us still here on Earth. I had a boy to raise, and he was turning into a damn fine man in front of me.

Intermission: PRACTICE

The winter Ollie played Squirt hockey was the snowiest season we'd seen since our family had moved to Hoosierland. Wave after wave of Arctic air rolled out of Canada, either pulling moisture off of Lake Michigan or chilling the wet storms that bubbled up from the Gulf. The white Christmas we'd enjoyed froze into a snow pack that only melted down to the bare lawns underneath for a single day in January. The thaw was followed by a quick squall that covered the city again. The wind howled out of the western plains and cut through Indiana, drifting and blowing the powder under skies of pale, skittering clouds. Hockey weather.

Two nights a week, one of us braved the snow to haul Oliver and his gear down to Pan Am Plaza in downtown Indy. Practice was scheduled at five thirty on Tuesdays, six thirty on Wednesdays. The attending parent prayed for a practice in the street-level rink. The basement pond was a freezing bunker, but the upstairs ice was surrounded by warm wooden bleachers and heaters for the spectators.

Pan American Plaza had been constructed in the 1980s specifically for the Pan American Games. Athletes from the Western Hemisphere had descended on Indy for a festival of amateur athletics, and the weight rooms and skating rinks remained after the games had ended.

The plaza was fronted by two blazing cauldrons and a wide, short staircase. Entering from the north end of the plaza, one passed between the buildings that housed the rinks and a low office complex. The cobbled walk opened onto a huge common area that surrounded a large fountain. The Colts hosted parties in the Plaza before every NFL home game, and the bricks around the fountain had seen numerous festivals throughout the years. The architecture around the Plaza ranged from the hundred-year-old brick facade of Union Station (the old train depot) to the utilitarian concrete that encased the RCA Dome. From the outside, Pan Am Plaza looked for all the world like a state-of-the-art winter sports facility. The interior was another issue.

Pan Am was a dump. The interior of the place looked like a third-world air raid shelter that had just been attacked by a U.S. fighter squadron—it had holes in the sheetrock, holes in the tiled drop ceilings, broken water fountains, and shattered glass and rotten boards around the ice. A fellow Ice hockey dad named Pete, a guy who never seemed to have a beef with anything or anybody, complained bitterly about the condition of the place. "You'd think they'd roll a little of my cash back into this joint," he'd honk in his Buffalo accent. "It's a damn disgrace."

It was. Parents who'd shelled out as much scratch as we had for our kids to play travel hockey didn't appreciate trudging through the ankle-deep puddles produced by the battered drinking fountains. The glass above the boards was so scratched and cloudy you could barely see your own kid playing the game if you stood rinkside. *Did a nickel of the cash we'd spent on ice time wind up in any kind of maintenance fund?* we wondered. We were embarrassed when visiting squads saw our home ice.

On the road, we would eyeball the other teams' facilities. We kept a close eye on how some of the other facilities in the larger cities looked—fresh paint, new glass, vending machines that didn't require a kick-punch-kick combination in just the right spots to deliver a Diet Coke. We understood that the state of our home rink was one thing that correctly called for a State of Righteous Indignation, especially for a facility in the very heart of a city the size of Indianapolis. Coaches, refs, and especially ten-year-olds made mistakes on and off the ice, but paying exorbitant rent to a slumlord merited a complaint.

When the temperature dropped into the single digits and stayed there for a few days, the uninsulated plumbing in the cellar below Pan Am's open, street-level plaza began to freeze and snap.

Water gushed out of the drop ceiling and into the hallways and snack bar downstairs. Mice began to appear, trying to outrun the deluge. The kids started naming them: Slayer, Taz, Shred. Amanda named one Pookie. The human Pookie punched her in the arm.

We complained, but nothing happened. The doors on the toilets hung on crookedly on their busted hinges, and the boards around the ice continued to rot. The parents slid into the rink across the wide, snow-covered plaza (the folks running Pan Am hardly ever shoveled it off), and the kids readied themselves amidst the crumbling wallboard in the locker rooms. The long, brutal winter, the perpetual clouds in the Indiana sky, and the condition of the Plaza all took their toll on the adults. Shouting matches between parent and parent—and an occasional confrontation between a parent and someone else's kid—became more and more commonplace. Tuesday practices meant someone was going to get out of line; Wednesday brought the inevitable apology.

The kids got cranky, too. One child melted down at the end of a practice, upset that a) everybody was popping him during scrimmage, and b) Cody didn't invite him to his birthday party (this, in the universe of the ten-year-old, is the ultimate dis). The evening ended with Angry Kid's Mom yelling at a few of his teammates and Coaches Mike and Mac waiting to chat with Angry Kid's Mom after everybody else had left for the night.

The coaches managed to defuse most of these incidents, but the general attitude of parental discontent was seeping into game situations. It manifested itself in a way that has affected both college and pro franchises in every sport. A clubhouse full of superstar egos always leads to a subpar performance by the team as a whole.

I noticed that Coach Mike had begun to step back during

practices. Coach Mac, who'd been working overtime throughout the season and hadn't been able to attend practices regularly, began to show up more often. Mike would stand back while Mac did the talking. The strategy seemed sound: Maybe the parents and kids who were blaming the team's league losses on Mike might give Mac a little more leeway and a little more respect.

Soon I realized that the problem wasn't the messenger, it was the message. Mike and Mac were realizing it, too. The coaches weren't going to get any respect unless they demanded it—loudly. Eventually, Coach Mac decided that enough was enough.

On a frosty Tuesday night, Mac stood before the players as they faced him in a line that stretched laterally across the rink on either side of the net. The parents watched as Mac laid it out.

"Y'all are gonna drill. If y'all screw up, y'all are gonna do it again. If y'all screw up again, y'all are gonna keep doin' it until y'all figger it out."

Mac started the evening with a firm but understated voice. Twenty minutes later, he was beet red.

"SPRINT!" yelled Mac. "GOAL LINE TO BLUE LINE, BACK, GOAL TO CENTER ICE, BACK, GOAL TO FAR BLUE, BACK, THEN END TO END AND STOP!"

This is called a "Herbie." It's the drill made famous by the late coach Herb Brooks, the guy who coached the 1980 U.S. Olympic team to a gold medal in Lake Placid.

The kids skated. Wheezing, they lined up for more directions. Mac was just getting wound up.

"What the hell is this half speed crap?" said Mac.

Cody made the mistake of protesting: "I wasn't going at ..." That was as far as he got.

"DON'T TALK BACK TO ME! You just bought the whole team a dozen more sprints! GO AGAIN!"

Halfway through the sprints, during which Mac yelled at the kids to pick up the pace the entire time, he let the kids rest for a moment. Not because he felt bad for them—just because he wanted to jaw at them some more.

"Last week Zack broke a scorin' slump. He put in a beauty. A great goal. I didn't see NONE O' YA tell him he did a good job. All you did was bitch about how he didn't pass. You whine about this kid or that kid. You whine about the refs. You don't help each other out. I DON'T KNOW WHY Y'ALL HATE EACH OTHER, BUT IT AIN'T HELPIN' THE TEAM."

Some of the parents who stood around the rink and watched this display tried to avoid eye contact with the other adults. This was the eight-hundred-pound gorilla in the living room that nobody mentioned. Mac knew why the kids criticized each other on the bench. Everybody knew the reason. Parents sniped about each other at home, and the kids took the attitude into the locker room and, subsequently, onto the ice.

Mac went on.

"I ain't drivin' two or three hours to BABYSIT you guys on the bench. You hear me? ACT LIKE A TEAM. TEAMS WIN GAMES. A BUNCH OF WHININ' BABIES ARE ONLY GONNA LOSE!"

The kids were shaking. Cold, fatigue, and terror set in all at once. They weren't prepping for a game against Dayton or Cincinnati. They weren't prepping for a shootout with the Soviet National Team of decades past. They might as well have been facing the Red Army on the Russian front in the winter of '44.

"If you wanna lose, go ahead. I'll bring a BOOK to read on the bench while y'all get outscored by a hundred points. BUT RIGHT NOW, Y'ALL ARE GONNA SKATE! GOAL LINE TO BLUE LINE, BACK ..." He repeated his directive.

Randy, Cody's dad, was standing near me during the tirade. Cody was furious for being called out. The kid was crying a little, tears of anger. Randy smiled. "That'll teach him," Randy confided.

"Yeah," I said, "that'll teach all of 'em. I'll bet you five bucks Oliver falls asleep in the car on the way home."

I would've lost the fiver. Oliver was absolutely torqued.

He hollered in the locker room. "We're a team! Yeah! Team! You wanna win, you gotta say TEAM! I am PART of this team. I am SPONGEBOB HOCKEYPANTS!" (Hey, the preadolescent brain is easily distracted by all the other junk floating around in its frontal lobes.)

Ollie jabbered all the way home. "Coach was right. Everybody whines too much. Babies don't win! I like Cody, but he's gotta keep his mouth shut. Don't mouth off to coach. That's bullshit!"

I gave the kid a sidelong glance in the rearview mirror from the driver's seat. He sat motionless in the back seat, suddenly realizing he dropped the s-bomb with an adult—no, his *dad*—within earshot. At the next red light, I turned around and stared at him. His eyes were big. I smiled and shook my head. "Watch your mouth yourself," I laughed. Oliver exhaled loudly. All I could think about was a holiday movie called *A Christmas Story* in which the main character, a boy named Ralphie who is around Ollie's age, screws up when he's changing a tire with his dad and unloads the f-word. Why does this always happen around the family car?

I had been in the passenger seat of my father's Opel GT at age eleven when I'd first cursed in front of my Dad. He was showing me the nifty way the headlights in his new ride were hidden until you needed them—and then magically rose out of the nose of the car when you turned them on. My reaction? "F---in' cool!" I couldn't watch TV for a week.

I didn't punish Ollie for his indiscretion. Frankly, I was happy he was so passionate about doing well.

I had a gift from Ollie that my father had never gotten from me. I was never all too athletic. I played, I tried, I was a gamer, but I was always second string, either riding the pines or being handed my walking papers during the second cut from the JV squad. I poured my energy into drawing and writing for a bunch of school publications. Sports became something for the high school jocks, and I had become an art room geek.

Oliver was strong. He wasn't very fast, but he played the game brilliantly. He knew his position, he knew how to slow down an offense, and he knew how to get in another guy's head. Ollie shoved and pushed and scrapped and frustrated an offense whenever it powered into his zone. His skating needed work and his stick handling was so-so, but he listened and learned every day. The coaches told me they loved Ollie's attitude. I was proud. Ollie—and everyone who saw him—knew he was just waiting for next year. Next year, next year when he'd be a Pee Wee, a year older, a kid who was allowed to *check*.

(CHECK, 1. *v.*—the term relating to the act of smackin' that son of a bitch wearing a different colored uniform and making him think twice about trying to score on us the next time he gets near this net, dammit. 2. *n.*—Pow!)

I also noticed Oliver was drifting into adolescence. Little girls began to call the house. Daily. He paid much more attention to beer commercials and lingerie ads. He was getting bigger—every day—and he was starting to smell really awful after a game or a practice. The kid also suffered from the occasional brain fart associated with a surge in hormones.

I'd send the boy to another floor to find something. He'd forget what he'd been sent for halfway up the stairs. I'd ask the child to lock our garage door; he'd open it, instead.

His mom and I got our biggest shock when his school pictures came in. Oliver's photos pictured him up on one knee, staring at the camera with half a determined smile. His eyes pierced the camera. He hunched forward toward the viewer. If you didn't know his actual height, you would've sworn this photo depicted a high school senior who'd had a close shave.

Ollie's face had narrowed; the baby fat was gone. He still played with his Micro Machines on the family room rug, he still called himself SpongeBob HockeyPants on a regular basis, he still got scared sometimes in the middle of the night, but all of these things had begun to take a backseat to his now constant interest in music and girls.

No longer interested in just the occasional blast of punk surging from a stereo, Oliver had taken to walking around with his head firmly sandwiched between a pair of earphones cabled to a personal CD player. He'd wander through the house or finish his social studies reading assignments while the faint sounds of percussion issued from either side of his skull. The punk was getting harder, louder, angrier, and a good bit filthier. I had to be even more vigilant about what the kid was listening to. He was moving beyond the Green Day and Ramones songs he'd recently discovered into some stuff that required a thorough listen by yours truly before the discs were released into his waiting hands.

I had actually begun to consider the relative value of the little sticker that was plastered on the front of seemingly every piece of music available for sale: PARENTAL ADVISORY— EXPLICIT CONTENT.

How explicit could we get? What degree of explicit was healthy for the kid to hear? The occasional swear word? A phrase about sex? A chorus about sex? A song about sex? Or drugs? Or murder?

Oliver insisted he could handle all of it. His mom insisted he could handle next to none of it. I fell somewhere in the middle. I wasn't terribly worried.

Either way, eventually I knew we'd lose this fight—soon Ollie would be at an age where he'd be able to purchase any piece of parentally frowned-upon metal his little heart desired. I was pretty sure that he had a decent moral foundation and wouldn't take the stuff literally. I figured I wouldn't wake up one cold night to find my progeny at the foot of my bed, eyes red and wild with the audio speed that had been pumped into his cerebral cortex, ready to stab me with one of his skates ...

Well, I hoped I wouldn't.

Nah. Despite what Oliver and his buds looked like to the opposition's parents, they were still ten-year-old kids adopting the mere adornments of high school kids. They weren't ready for shop class, liquor, and jail quite yet.

When Ollie and the rest of the Junior Ice—the Purple Gang, all dressed in their matching pullovers—rolled into an arena, they looked for all the world like some kind of semi-pro squad. Same black jeans, same Junior Ice ball caps turned around backward or sideways, half of them dragging a wheeled hockey bag with one hand while carrying a Sony Discman in the other. Some were skate-punkin' like Ollie, some were walking with the slow roll and attitude of a wannabe gangsta rapper. They'd straggle into the locker room, drop the gear, set their sticks in a corner by the door, hand the personal sound system to Mom, and immediately morph back into little kids.

The Purple Gang would go running through the hallways of whatever arena it was visiting, yelping like a pack of small dogs. The kids would crowd around the vending machines, every one of them insistent on buying that last bag of Skittles, muscling each other around and jockeying for position in front of the dollar slot. They'd yell and push and call each other "girl," but they were all teetering on the edge of maturity. A few of the younger kids had another year ahead of them at the Squirt level, but most would go marching into the Pee Wee division next season.

The kids who were serious about hockey would be attending "checking camp" in the summertime. It would be required of them if they wanted to continue to the next level. They'd be taught how to give and receive a hit. They wouldn't be taught how to sneak an arm around a date in a dark movie theater. They'd have to learn all of that painful stuff on their own.

They'd also learn that Mom and Dad weren't always right. A bunch of them had a sneaking suspicion already—they knew, secretly, that Mom and Dad were making all this up as they went along. There wasn't any Great Book of Mom and Dad Wisdom to refer to. There wasn't anyone giving Mom and Dad the answers to the questions that came up every day. Coach might be right, and the people who made you dinner might be wrong. Soon, they'd start to question everything we told them. They'd do what they wanted to do and make decisions for themselves. They'd be listening to their compact discs with all the dirty words intact.

RESUME PLAY

On the second weekend in February, we were booked for a four-game stand in the Buckeye state. We had a 1:30 game in Oxford at Miami University of Ohio on Saturday, followed by a 5:30 game in Hamilton, just north of Cincinnati. After the second game, we'd be driving to Columbus for a Sunday doubleheader against the Junior Bluejackets.

I spent Saturday morning packing our stuff while Amy ran

errands. She shipped off a box of clothes to her brother's family, full of stuff Oliver had seemingly outgrown in a single month. She also tried to take our Christmas tree to Broad Ripple Park so it could be recycled into mulch.

The tree had been sitting in its stand on our front porch since December 26. It was weird at first, seeing the very same tree that had been covered in garland and lights standing bare out there in the elements, but soon it became a permanent fixture. The needles clung tenaciously to the branches, and the damn thing stayed green for the entire month of January. Every weekend we tried to carve out time to get the tree to the recycling dropoff point, and every weekend we simply ran out of time. Two full-time jobs, bass lessons, travel hockey—the tree waited patiently while we ran all over the Midwest.

Finally, Amy shoved the tree into the back of the station wagon on a Saturday morning and drove to Broad Ripple Park. Sure, we could've thrown in the towel and hauled the tree to the curb where the local sanitation engineer would've thrown it atop a pile of other crap and hauled it off to a landfill, but we *recycle*. Suburban liberals like us *recycle*. (It's easier than taking petitions door to door or campaigning for our chosen candidates.)

Indy's recycling program is voluntary, and it costs participants directly. You pay the recycling company a ten-dollar monthly fee, and the company issues your home a bright red bin for your cans and bottles and newspapers. They empty the bin every day that regular trash pickup occurs. The recycling guy leaves the bin in an upside-down position in the exact spot where he found it. The regular state-paid garbage men usually leave our plastic trashcan in the middle of the street.

The recycling folks don't pick up trees. If you want the city to turn your tree into mulch for one of its many urban parks, you had to do some hauling yourself. Amy rolled up to the drop-off point in the parking lot of Broad Ripple Park and was greeted by a pile of brown needles and a sign on a post. The sign read:

TREE RECYCLING ENDS JANUARY 31.

Amy threw the tree in a dumpster behind the park's staff building.

After Amy finished her crime, we left at 11 a.m., driving east through Indiana on I-70, then taking old U.S. 27 south through the low hills of the Indiana/Ohio border region just north of the Ohio River. White farmhouses dotted the snowy, rolling landscape around us, the silver tops of silos reflecting the cold blues and grays of the land and sky. The country bore a striking resemblance to rural western New York, where Amy spent her childhood summers in towns with names like East Otto and Salamanca.

We were near the border towns of College Corner and West College Corner. Even though most of the Hoosier state is in the Eastern Standard Time zone, Indiana didn't spring forward or fall back then. For half the year, College Corner and West College Corner were in two different time zones. The local high school that serves the two towns actually straddles the state line, and each half of the school's basketball court was in a different state. During the summer months, a kid could throw a ball inbounds at 3 p.m. on the western end of the court and pass it to a kid waiting on the eastern side at 4 p.m.

We got off the Interstate in Richmond, Indiana, a town that had once been the center for recorded jazz in America. For a brief period of time early in the recording industry, Richmond boasted the finest studios in the world. Jazz and blues players came from Chicago and New Orleans to make discs in this town. Some of Louis Armstrong's early stuff was preserved here.

Just outside of town we encountered the other big influence in this part of our country: the headquarters of a Christian publication called the *Endtimes Newspaper*. "If you buy a subscription to the *Endtimes Newspaper*," Amy asked, "will they take a check?"

We pulled into the parking lot of Goggin Arena on the Miami of Ohio University campus at around 12:30. The lobby of the Goggin featured an elevated seating area that surrounded a freestanding fireplace. A big-screen TV was tuned to CNN. The post-September 11 Terror Alert system had been elevated to Code Orange, which meant High Alert. Orange was, of course, second only to Code Red. Code Red meant that something somewhere was being attacked. Most of the Junior Ice did not know this. The Junior Ice knew that Code Red was a kind of Mountain Dew.

On that particular day the announcer on CNN told us that the United Nations was hunting for weapons in Iraq, North Korea probably had a missile that could fly a nuclear bomb into Los Angeles, and the Attorney General of the United States wanted all Americans to stock up on plastic sheeting, duct tape, and canned goods.

I said to Amy, "the *Endtimes Newspaper* is currently *not* accepting checks."

The Purple Gang ran through the hallways after they dumped their gear in the locker room. The Goggin was painted red to honor Miami's NCAA hockey team, the Redhawks. Banners from the CCHA college league hung over the spectators' benches in the Goggin. The Redhawks were in elite company: They played squads from hockey-mad schools like Michigan and Michigan State, Northern and Western Michigan Universities, Alaska-Fairbanks, and Lake Superior College. Banners from Notre Dame, Ohio State, Ferris State, and Bowling Green rounded out the competition.

A photo collage in the lobby gave an indication of the talent the Redhawks managed to draw. A framed series of portraits reading "Redhawks in the Pros" held the headshots of two dozen recent graduates who'd turned ice hockey into a full-time job. Most of the guys were sticking in minor-league cities in Canada and the United States. A kid with the familiar name of Robitaille had been playing for the NHL's Pittsburgh Penguins, and a man named Savage was part of the Phoenix Coyotes. One standout had returned to his homeland to play for Finland's national team.

We were in hardcore hockey country. The Butler County Blackhawks Squirt A team was undefeated in our league. The Blackhawks were big, fast, and powerful.

Our coaches lined up on the bench with the Ice. Mac, Mike, and Ken, the team manager, manned the doors leading from the bench onto the ice. Pete was again recruited to man the penalty box for the Purple Gang. It was his nearly painless job to open the door and let a player free when the player's penalty time ran out. Pete had a bandana on his head (as always) and was wearing a black trench coat to keep warm. He looked like a guy who'd gone to a Phish concert only to be somehow drafted by the Mafia while he was partying in the parking lot.

We waved to Pete in the bleachers. He waved back. The Ice starters took their positions. So did the Blackhawks. The ref dropped the puck. The Blackhawks scored immediately.

So it went. We watched an absolute thumping of our kids by the Blackhawks. Oliver went after a puck and crashed into the boards, then fell as the puck skittered into the hands of the Blackhawks. "Don't check yourself, son," I said aloud. Everybody around me began laughing. Jeremy was hit with a tripping call. He spent two minutes in the box with his dad.

"Nothing like a little quality father-and-son time!" said Pete's wife, Jenny.

Our team was going to lose. The parents were taking it in stride. The Butler County Blackhawks were simply a better squad.

Midway through the second period, with the score 3–0, I left the rink to use the men's room. When I came back, the scoreboard read:

HOME: 4

VISITOR: 0

PENALTY: 74—1:46

There's nothing like stepping back into a rink and seeing your son's number on the penalty tally. Ollie had apparently clobbered some kid—checking in a non-checking league—while I'd been taking a leak. Pretty soon, the Ice would have two men in the penalty box and the score would rise to 5–0.

The Ice played hard, but superior talent won out. The defense couldn't stop the 'Hawks, and the offense couldn't seem to put one into the net. The game ended 6–0.

The next game was in Hamilton, Ohio, against this very same team.

We'd been hearing rumors about the Hamilton rink all day. One of the Hawks' parents had confirmed our suspicions: The Hamilton rink was outdoors.

The Hamilton ice rink was covered by a curved wooden roof that was supported by steel struts. It was completely open at both ends, giving the place the look of an unfinished Quonset hut. One of the long sides of the rink was blocked in by a small lobby with a concession stand, locker rooms, and a hooded fireplace. The bottom six feet of the other long side was open to the elements. One short end was outfitted with a series of tilted fabric baffles that looked like the wings of some turn-of-the-century flying machine that never made it off the ground. The baffles didn't seem to stop the wind that howled through the rink at a steady fifteen miles per hour.

I stood outside next to Coach Mac, regarding the place. "I used to play here when I was a kid," he told me. "They've fixed the place up—new scoreboard, and looks like they finally put some glass in."

"No glass?" I asked, seeing visions of hockey parents past leaning over the boards only to be met with a rubber biscuit to the skull.

"Used to be chainlink even on the spectators' side." Mac pointed across the rink to the long end that opened onto a wooded tract of land. Sure enough, chainlink fence above the boards kept the puck within the confines of the game.

"These Blackhawks are, uh, tough," I noted to Mac as I stared in disbelief at the fencing.

"Yeah—they didn't field a Double-A Squirt team this year down here. These Blackhawks ain't a Single-A team. They're older; they've got more experience than all that. That's why nobody beats 'em in Single-A. I don't think it's fair, but I ain't callin' the shots."

Mac was not one to gripe about another team's prowess. I was sure he hadn't told the kids any of this. In Mac's universe, the situation was what it was. You didn't bitch, you just went out and played your best.

I ducked into the battered lobby to warm up. The wall that faced the rink had windows in it, and below the windows were stacks and stacks of firewood. Kids and adults rubbed their hands by the hood that hung suspended over the big metal fireplace in the middle of the room. Low wooden benches surrounded it. Jenny and Pete had brought a huge thermos full of mulled cider, and Pete had added a little rum to his serving. Parents here and there were drinking beers on the sly, and Amy and I took the occasional nip from a small flask of scotch we'd brought. The folks staffing the *Endtimes Newspaper* would have disapproved.

Hamilton's locker rooms were tiny, six-by-ten-foot closets warmed by an over-efficient heater suspended from the ceiling. Spend ten minutes in this sauna and you'd emerge drenched in sweat. Half the kids had simply opted to change out in the lobby, going into the men's room if they had to pull off their skivvies for any reason. A sign next to the doors that led from the lobby to the rink read:

"PLEASE DO NOT DIG HOLES IN ICE."

When had this been a problem? I wondered. *Had somebody confused the rink for an ice-fishing shack?*

 **Time-Out:** THE RINKS

It's occurred to me that at this point you've probably made the assumption that the average hockey rink is so loathsome and nightmarish a place that even Faust himself could not have imagined its horrors. Well, you're right. Some of the rinks that serve the youth sport are portals to hell.

Ellenberger Park in Indianapolis was an old outdoor rink that was surrounded by an unheated metal pole building about twenty years ago. This structure had the unique ability to create a sheltered environment that was actually colder indoors than out. At one point during Oliver's first travel season, the cooling unit that kept the skating surface frozen malfunctioned, and the ice melted. A look at a thermometer that hung inside the rink revealed an otherworldly fact: The air temperature inside Ellenberger was, at the time when the rink turned to liquid, twenty-five degrees. Hold on to your hats, fans of quantum physics, purveyors of wormholes in the space-time continuum, believers in little green men and cold fusion: *The skating surface at Ellenberger was actually warmer than the interior of the building itself.*

Another marvelous dump is the Hara Arena in Dayton, Ohio. I'm pretty sure that the folks who made the movie *Slap Shot* might've considered this facility as a location but dismissed the joint as "too rugged." Hara resembles Indy's Pepsi Coliseum—after it had been picked up and moved to, say, the South Bronx and then abandoned for ten years. The ceiling over the main rink seems to have at one time been covered with square metal panels, most of which have since fallen down. In fact, a few of those panels are still currently in the process of falling down—some dangle precariously overhead, twisting gently in the frosty drafts drifting through the great unheated cavern, those deadly sheets of steel hanging by only a bent screw or a bit of wire. Watch where you're sittin', Damocles.

There are, however, a great many exceptions.

One such exception is McMillen Ice Arena in Fort Wayne, Indiana. The rink is part of McMillen Park, which seems to have been named after Dale and Agnes McMillen. This is just an educated guess on my part, since there's little more to clue you in than a picture of the elderly McMillen couple hanging in the lobby of the rink. Dale and Agnes have huge grins on their faces, and they're holding what seem to be empty goblets of wine. I don't know if the grins and the glasses are related, but the McMillens sure do look like people you'd have wanted to party with.

The joint is big, clean, and, most important, warm. You can actually take your coat off while you're watching a game and feel comfortable. The concession stand is always loaded with goodies, and the lobby has a fireplace and two TV sets you can watch in the hour or so of downtime between your kid's back-to-back hockey games. (Or if Indiana University is playing Purdue, you might be watching TV *during* your kid's hockey game.)

Fort Wayne is also populated by some of the friendliest hockey parents in the state. (Maybe it's got something to do with all the strip joints in town.) Once, during a break between two games, the parents of the host team treated the Indy players and parents to a spaghetti dinner they'd catered in from a local restaurant. Fort Wayne's coach stood up after the meal and pointed to a GLM (good-looking mom) in a pink-and-black sweatsuit.

"Linda set this up," he said, "but let's give a big round of applause for all the Fort Wayne moms!"

The Fort Wayne moms gave the guy a look that read: *Applause is lovely, but it ain't gonna wipe up all the tomato sauce that these little goons have splattered on the linoleum, bub.*

The high end of the spectrum for youth hockey, however, resides in Westfield, Indiana. A rink called the Arctic Zone features lasers, a pumping sound system, and a balcony that gives the spectator a terrific view of the game below. During one of Ollie's games, I sat at a barstool next to a high table in the balcony and noticed a bowl of pretzels and peanuts in the middle of the table.

Furtively, I glanced about. I snuck a handful. No one complained. I scooped up another handful. No cries of, "Git yer hand outta my muchies!" were issued. I emptied the bowl. Immediately a waitress showed up to refill the snacks. "Would you like a soda or a beer from the bar?" she asked.

I laughed. A beer.

A beer. Why, what a prankster. She even had a tray full of empties to complete the ...

Are you kidding me? I'm watching youth hockey and I can buy beer here?

She sensed my incredulity. "Miller, Bud, or Coors?" she asked, walking slowly back to a door at the rear of the balcony.

I turned around. Behind me, through a door and on the other side of a plate-glass window, was a bar resplendent with tables and chairs, burgers and dogs, Pepsi and brewskis, and a flat-screen HDTV broadcasting an NFL game. Parents sat here and there enjoying a cold one while kids between games played knee hockey in the hallway. (More about knee hockey later.)

Sure, there are times, when it's cold, like in Hamilton, that the occasional nip is allowed. After a game, especially when you've just witnessed a tough loss for the team, it may be polite to buy a case of cold ones and invite the coaches to tip as many as they care to. But the actual sanctioning of beer consumption during youth hockey through sales designed to bring in more cash for the rink—well, folks, that's a new one to a Hoosier like me.

On the downside, the crankiness of your average hockey parent can obviously be amplified with a few cans of suds. On the upside, fundrasing through alcohol sales beats the heck out of selling decorator candles to your coworkers. I'll take the risk.

RESUME PLAY

When the game at Hamilton started, I went back outside to watch the game from the bleachers. The sun began to set, and streaks of light filtered onto the ice from one of the open semicircles of the curved roof. Since the rink was outdoors and the temperature was in the twenties, the ice was hard, which gave the players a fast skating surface. This played into the Blackhawks' game plan nicely—their speed seemed to triple on the quicker surface.

Some parents huddled under blankets as the Blackhawks delivered another beating to the Junior Ice. Amy and I stood on the top row of the bleachers, stamping our feet and yelling encouragement. At one point, Pete, assigned to penalty box duty again, waved to Jenny across the ice and pointed to his bare hands. He'd forgotten his gloves. To get in or out of the penalty box one had to make a trip across the ice. Between periods, Jenny summoned her son to the glass on the spectators' side. She threw the gloves over the glass and yelled to Jeremy: "Take those to your father!"

Pete held up his hands after Jeremy delivered the gloves. The entire rink gave him a round of applause.

There wasn't much else to cheer for if you were rooting for Indy. Our team wasn't able to score a single goal in six periods. The game ended with a 5–0 final score.

I'd been careful not to drink much during the game. We had a ninety-minute drive to Columbus ahead of us, so I'd had a fair amount of the terrible coffee that the Hamilton concession stand sold at the bargain price of fifty cents per cup. We left the venue at about 7 p.m., had a charming spousal argument regarding the best route to take northeast as we hunted for a road out of Hamilton, and finally settled on trying to locate I-71. This required a ten-mile trip across a two-lane country highway through the towns of Otterbein and Lebanon, which caused my wife to repeat the question: "Are you sure this is the right way?" every twenty-seven seconds.

We found the interstate and then realized we were starving. We'd been hoping for a nice sit-down meal when we rolled into Columbus, but our guts were dictating otherwise. Oliver hollered out: "I see a Wendy's!" and we pulled off the highway and into the drive-thru. Another Saturday with the Indy Junior Ice, another meal in the car. My burger slid apart as I tried to hold it with one hand and steer with the other. It never failed. Every road trip ended with the same ritual: Dad fishing condiment-covered tomatoes and onions out of his lap. Half of my pants had been ruined by the disconcerting appearance of ketchup stains on the flies.

We pulled into the Marriott in Dublin, Ohio, at about nine o'clock that night.

The Columbus suburb of Dublin is the home of a huge sports facility that includes indoor and outdoor fields for soccer and track, hockey rinks, football fields, and baseball diamonds. Our hotel was full of kids and adults from all over the Midwest who were in town for a travel soccer tournament that same weekend. As we hauled our gear to the room, we saw signs encouraging the Toledo Stingers and the Dayton Wildcats. What? No Youngstown Mobsters? No Cleveland Flaming River Rats?

A soccer mom gaped in awe at Oliver as he trundled down the hall toward our room, his equipment bag trailing behind him. "Good Lord!" she exclaimed. "What are you carrying?"

"Hockey pads!" Oliver replied briskly.

The woman looked at Amy and me. "You poor people," she said.

"You don't know the half of it," said Amy.

A number of Junior Ice moms and dads began to congregate in Pete and Jenny's room. We found their digs after we dropped our stuff off in our room. A few adults were draining beers, and some were drinking wine out of coffee mugs or bathroom glasses. Coach Mac regaled us with tales about his father-in-law, who was also his hunting and fishing buddy.

One night when Mac's pop by marriage had been too blasted to drive home from an afternoon of bass fishing, Mac had pinched the old man's keys and slid behind the wheel. The old man didn't want to go home just then, but Mac insisted, telling the coot he was too inebriated to be running around in public. The fight escalated until Mac finally snapped: "Well, if you don't like it, just get out and walk, then!" The old man said that would suit him just fine, and proceeded to exit the vehicle. Trouble was, the car was traveling at about thirty miles per hour at that particular moment.

The old man hit the pavement and rolled. Mac then heard a muffled thump as the right rear tire of his car ran over the old man's legs.

Mac pulled the car over and got our to see if the geezer had survived. He was prepared for the worst: broken bones, even some terrible life-threatening injury. He didn't expect to see his father-in-law jogging toward the car and yelling. "Run over me again, ya son of a bitch, and I'll hit ya so hard yer grandmama's gonna feel it!" Perhaps the old man had been incredibly relaxed from the booze, or maybe it was just the angle at which he'd been struck, but Mac's father-in-law suffered only a few bruises and nothing else.

You could see why the kids were a little scared of Coach Mac. After all, he had run over somebody he called "Dad."

The stories drifted on into the night. The kids set up a knee hockey game in the hallway outside Pete and Jenny's room. The night manager arrived to break up their game when the soccer people began complaining. Half an hour later, the manager returned to announce that we adults were now the problem: a dozen hockey moms and dads whooping it up in a hotel room designed for four people was annoying the other guests.

The party broke up about midnight. The next day's first game didn't start until noon.

Time-Out: THE HOCKEY DIET REDUX

I would like to pause briefly at this point in my narrative to offer a word of thanks.

To the man, woman, or group of individuals who invented

the breakfast buffet: You have my eternal gratitude.

Where else can the hungry traveler encounter a five-gallon tub of scrambled eggs? Twelve dozen flapjacks? Seven pounds of sausage? A barrel of bacon? Enough syrup to send an entire family into a diabetic coma?

Where else can one find Belgian waffles and Froot Loops living in perfect harmony alongside cantaloupe and Special K?

Sure, sometimes there's a line at the toaster. Sure, sometimes a four-year-old sneezes into a steamer tray full of hash browns. Sure, your server expects a tip even though you're doing all the work. Still—where else can you eat *exactly* the right amount of food—and then go back for seconds?

RESUME PLAY

We ate at the buffet on Sunday morning and then made our way to The Chiller, a spectacular skating facility in the middle of the Dublin amateur sports complex. The Chiller has two rinks, one for youth games and another for everything else: figure skating, public skating, you name it. When we arrived, a bunch of guys were playing a pick-up hockey game for folks ages forty and up. They skated at about three-quarter speed and didn't check, but they seemed to be shooting the puck as hard as they possibly could.

The Chiller is also a part-time practice rink for the Columbus Blue Jackets, Ohio's only NHL team. The pro shop features dozens of fleeces, shirts, and jerseys bearing the Blue Jackets' logo. Cities with major-league hockey teams always have strong youth hockey programs. I was concerned about a long, demoralizing weekend for the Indy Junior Ice Squirt A Travel Hockey team.

Ollie and his team began suiting up. The coach had to chase Erica out of the locker room. This was becoming more and more common.

Erica was Tyler's older sister. (Tyler was a forward on the Ice.) Erica knew what everybody was doing and where everybody was. Erica knew whose parents were divorced, whose parents were thinking about divorcing, and whose parents were simply fighting. Erica knew who got along with who, who hated who, and who pretended to like someone she really couldn't stand. Erica roamed the halls of the hotels when the team was on the road, listening at doorways and watching what rooms the adults would visit. Erica always made an appearance in the locker room before and after every game. Oliver called her "Erica the Spy."

Erica the Spy appeared at my side as I watched the forty-plus game.

"I hear these parents from the other team think we play too rough," she announced.

"Really?" I replied. "Where'd that come from?" Erica the Spy had her redeeming qualities.

"It's been going around. Somebody's mom from Columbus heard it from her sister in Cincinnati. The Ice are mean." Erica the Spy wandered off again.

Amazing, I thought. Why couldn't the CIA recruit people like Erica? Osama bin Laden would've been in U.S. custody on September 12, 2001.

The Chiller's two rinks were separated by a long block of locker rooms. A platform above the locker rooms served as an observation balcony for both rinks. I climbed the stairs to the balcony as the first game got underway. I had a bird's-eye view of the entire rink. Across the ice, the Columbus parents sat in a stand of gleaming aluminum bleachers. Within the first two minutes, Erica the Spy's brother Tyler took a pass from Jared and put it into the net. The Junior Ice scoring drought ended.

The balcony was an amazing vantage point. Beyond the

terrific view, the vaulted ceiling of The Chiller carried sound from both benches and the field of play and projected it onto the platform. I could hear every complaint from the coaches and every insult the players exchanged. The most popular? "You skate like a girl!" This was pretty ineffective when directed at our Amanda.

The Ice and the Junior Blue Jackets were evenly matched. The two teams traded goals back and forth through the first game. Erica the Spy's information had been accurate regarding the Columbus parents: Their group complained bitterly about the bumps the Junior Ice delivered to the opposition. The Columbus crew screamed at the refs in fury. The refs were allowing a good deal of "incidental contact." Oliver was slamming into people left and right, but he didn't seem to draw a single call.

In addition to being physical, the Ice were playing well. They passed the puck instead of trying to play the hero alone. They looked before they passed. They played for position, not glory. Matt, the goalie, stopped most of the forty shots that came his way. Down briefly in the third period, the Ice didn't quit. The final: Ice 5, Blue Jackets 4.

A Columbus dad with a thick Canadian accent walked past me after the game. "Good physical match, eh?" he said.

I smiled. "Yeah. You from Columbus?"

"Live here now. From Edmonton originally," he replied.

"Wow," I said. "Oilers. Gretzky."

"You betcha. Hey, good goalie you got there, eh?" He clapped me on the shoulder and walked away.

Erica the Spy appeared at my side again. She pointed at the dad who had just been talking to me. "That man is originally from Canada," she said.

"I heard," I told her.

We had an hour to kill between games. I sat at a table by the concession stand and the skate rental desk taping Oliver's stick. Ollie liked the blade wrapped with fresh tape before every game. This was the last task he still allowed me to complete for him before his matches. The laces were now his own personal chore, but only Dad could wrap his stick with the perfect half-lap tape job that gave a player more control of the puck. The fabric tape gave a slight cushion to the blade and provided friction so that the biscuit was easier to handle.

As I wrapped the blade, I saw a sign on the wall of The Chiller: "TELL US! Has one of our employees done something great for you today?"

Hmm, I thought. The kid behind the concession counter didn't drop a load of nacho cheese into my fake cappuccino. Way to go, Columbus! You've got one up on the snack bar in Indy! I made a mental note to mention this stalwart service to The Chiller's management.

The kids ate pizza and soft pretzels at the tables around me. Two of our players, both wearing soaking-wet T-shirts and hockey pants, played War with a deck of cards emblazoned with the images of the Indiana Pacemates, the cheerleading squad for Indy's NBA franchise. A few kids drifted past me on Cruisers, tennis shoes with pop-out wheels that turn the footwear into skates. A knot of Indy parents chatted with one another. All the kids ignored them except for Erica the Spy, who listened to their conversation intently.

Jared walked by Erica. Erica liked Jared, so she punched him in the arm. Jared punched back. Jared's dad yelled at him for hitting a girl. The other kids laughed at Jared for getting yelled at.

Ollie chased John Michael through the snack bar. The two of them then wandered over to the pro shop and bought something called "stick wax." Cody spilled ketchup down the front of his jersey. Zack relived his game-winning goal, repeating the story to anyone who'd listen. After a bit, I began to ignore the kids and started eyeing the Junior Ice parents. All of the Indy adults seemed to be getting along with one another. It couldn't have happened at a better time. The regular season was almost over.

FEBRUARY—3rd PERIOD

The Indy Junior Ice Squirt A Travel Hockey team lost the second game of its double-header with the Columbus Junior Blue Jackets by a final score of 6–4. Despite the win, most of the Columbus moms and dads were fairly upset with Indy's style of play. They thought our kids hit too hard and too often.

Amy noticed that there was a direct correlation between the amount of pre-game pampering a team's parents gave their kids and the number of complaints those same parents had about hitting. "When I saw all the moms and dads from Columbus hauling their kids' hockey bags in, I knew there'd be trouble," she said.

She was right. Our kids generally handled their own gear. Our crew whined about a good many things, but physicality wasn't one of them. The Ice liked a game full of hits.

 **Time-Out:** THE HOCKEY DAD'S DAD

While we were in Ohio, one of the stories that was garnering national attention involved a kid named LeBron James, a basketball phenom from Cleveland who was sure to be drafted directly out of high school by the NBA. LeBron's mom had managed to wrangle an auto loan for a Hummer worth somewhere in the neighborhood of seventy-five thousand dollars, even though she didn't seem to have a job. The bank had loaned her the money since her boy was soon to become a multi-millionaire, and she had given the vehicle to her son. James had also received some gifts from a local sporting goods store, a fact that had disqualified him from playing for his high school team until a judge intervened on the kid's behalf.

I wondered when a scout had first gotten an eyeful of James. At ten? Twelve? Fourteen years old? When had the talent hunters decided that James didn't need to develop his skills at Duke or Connecticut? When had the agent stepped in and told him to skip academia and get right down to raking in the Benjamins?

I'd heard rumblings from some of the parents I knew who had kids on the Double-A Ice squads: Oliver could've been better. Should've had more skating lessons, should've gone to more camps.

I began to wonder—had we pissed away last summer? We'd gone on vacation in Northern Michigan. Should the money we'd spent on renting a house by a lake have been better used on some kind of backward-skating/stick-handling/contract-negotiation-training overnight camp? How much hockey was too much hockey?

I tried to shake off my doubts as quickly as they appeared. There was one immutable fact in my favor: Oliver wasn't bored. Hockey wasn't a job. One February weekend we were scheduled for a pair of games against the Columbus, Indiana, Flames in Pan Am Plaza. Ollie woke with a hundred-degree fever, chills, and a sore throat. He insisted he wanted to play that day despite the fact that he could barely swallow a chewable Tylenol.

Amy and I had argued over the wisdom of letting the kid play hockey. He wanted to go, the team needed him, and if he was sick already, what difference would two hours of exercise make? I told my wife that if the boy felt well enough to play, he should play. Amy disagreed, using a few choice words—all of which ended in "hole." A snowstorm settled the issue—the opposing team had cancelled its trip to Indy two hours before face-off.

Ollie loved hockey. He wasn't going through the motions just to please me. That meant he'd had just the right amount of ice time. Right?

Didn't it? Or was his passion insatiable? Could the kid hold up through a summer of camp after camp, workshop after workshop? Was I giving the kid enough? I didn't want to be a sports-mad parent shoving his child toward some unattainable dream. But I didn't want Ollie to miss a single chance for glory, either.

Ollie was sick in bed in the days that followed Valentine's Day. Saturday it snowed; Sunday it snowed some more. Indiana was being hammered by one of the worst winters ever. Every morning I shoveled off the driveway and wondered if I was doing enough for my boy. The wind swept the snow into drifts and eddies around me as I scraped and dug. But I had to clear a path for the car. We had to go to work and bass lessons and hockey practice. Hockey practice.

That weekend, in between bouts with the ever-falling snow, I talked to my father on the phone. Dad, an attorney in Baltimore, told me to keep up the good work with Oliver.

"We got all the pictures you sent," he said. "The ones from hockey were my favorites. You keep after my grandson. You never know when a scout might show up for a look."

I held the phone away from my ear and stared at the receiver in disbelief. My own father! My own dear ol' dad wanted *more* from that young man, expected Oliver to live up to his *full potential*. What was I missing? Ten-year-olds weren't supposed to be making career decisions! I hadn't stumbled across my true calling until I was seven years out of college! Scouts? Scouts? Please.

Scouts. Who could deny that the kid constantly talked about playing hockey for the Michigan Wolverines?

Scouts. Ollie's heroes weren't rock stars or skateboarders. They had names like Hull and Chelios, and they almost always wore the red and white you found in Detroit.

Scouts.

At some point during that snowy weekend, I told Amy that Oliver needed all the hockey instruction we could afford. The kid had some talent and an overwhelming passion, and he deserved as many of our resources as we could humanly offer. To my surprise, Amy agreed.

Intermission: LINGO

The Buckeye Tournament was approaching, as was the Indiana State Tournament. I decided I needed to bone up on my hockey lingo; God save the Hockey Dad who yelled the wrong thing at the wrong time. I began surfing the Web in earnest, looking to solidify my knowledge of the game before the championship series began. What follows are the fruits of my research, footnoted and annotated. Infractions include the Proper Coach's Commentary and the Opposing Parent Psycho Heckle. The former is an example of the kind of constructive criticism or compliment that you should issue from your child's bench; the latter is what some schmuck who's rooting for the other team is likely to say to your ten-year-old.

OFFSIDES: "Players of an attacking team may not precede the puck into the attacking zone." (USA Hockey Official Playing Rules 2001–2003)

> **Proper Coach's Commentary:** "Be aware of where your teammates are on the ice."
>
> **Opposing Parent Psycho Heckle:** "Too bad your seeing eye dog can't skate with ya!"

ICING: "For the purpose of this rule, the center red line will divide the ice into halves. Should any player of a team, equal or superior in numerical strength to the opposing team, shoot, bat with the hand or stick, kick or deflect the puck from his own half of the ice, beyond the goal line of the opposing team, play shall be stopped and the puck faced-off at the end zone face-off spot of the offending team." (USA Hockey Official Playing Rules 2001–2003)

> **Proper Coach's Commentary:** "Be aware of where your teammates are on the ice."
>
> **Opposing Parent Psycho Heckle:** "Next time ya might wanna pass it to somebody who's there!"

HOLDING: "No player shall impede the progress of an opponent by using his hands … or any other means." (USA Hockey Official Playing Rules 2001–2003)

> **Proper Coach's Commentary:** "Be aware of where your opponents are on the ice."
>
> **Opposing Parent Psycho Heckle:** "What time's the prom?"

HOOKING: "No player shall impede the progress of an opponent by using the stick." (USA Hockey Official Playing Rules 2001–2003)

> **Proper Coach's Commentary:** "Be aware of where your opponents are on the ice."
>
> **Opposing Parent Psycho Heckle:** "What time's the fishin' tournament?"

HIGH-STICKING: "The carrying of sticks above the normal height of the shoulder is prohibited. The referee may assess a minor or a major penalty on any player violating this rule." (USA Hockey Official Playing Rules 2001–2003)

> **Proper Coach's Commentary:** "Be aware of where your stick is when you're on the ice."
>
> **Opposing Parent Psycho Heckle:** "Yo! Tiger Woods!"

TRIPPING: "A minor penalty shall be imposed on any player who shall place his stick, foot, arm, hand, or elbow in such a manner that it shall cause his opponent to trip or fall." (USA Hockey Official Playing Rules 2001–2003)

> **Proper Coach's Commentary:** "Be aware of where your stick is when you're on the ice."
>
> **Opposing Parent Psycho Heckle:** "Yo! Tiger Woods!"

SLASHING: "Referees should penalize as 'slashing' any player who swings his stick at any opposing player (whether in or out of range) without actually striking him or where a player on the pretext of playing the puck makes a wild swing at the puck with the object of intimidating an opponent." (USA Hockey Official Playing Rules 2001–2003)

> **Proper Coach's Commentary:** "Be aware of where your stick

is when you're on the ice."

Opposing Parent Psycho Heckle: "Yo! Tiger Woods!"

INTERFERENCE: "A minor penalty shall be imposed on a player who interferes with or impedes the progress of an opponent who is not in possession of the puck." (USA Hockey Official Playing Rules 2001-2003)

> **Proper Coach's Commentary:** "Be aware of where the puck is when you're on the ice."
>
> **Opposing Parent Psycho Heckle:** "Yo! Dick Butkus!"

MISCONDUCT: "A 'MISCONDUCT' penalty involves the removal of a player, other than a goalkeeper, from the game for a period of ten minutes, but another player is permitted to immediately replace a player so removed. A player or Team Official incurring a 'GAME MISCONDUCT' penalty shall be suspended for the next one game of that team." (USA Hockey Official Playing Rules 2001–2003)

> **Proper Coach's Commentary:** "Be aware of where your head is when you're on the ice."
>
> **Opposing Parent Psycho Heckle:** "Hey, Ma—what time is Junior's next parole hearing?"

As far as penalties go, there's also "Checking in a Non-Checking League"—which was Ollie's favorite infraction. The "accidental" check occurred at least once per game during the 2002–2003 season. It usually started when an overexcited defenseman, trained to concentrate on the *man* and not the *puck*, used all his energy to stop the *man*—whether he had the puck or not.

The terms that define legal stuff could get pretty confusing, too. Here's a rundown:

BREAKAWAY: There's nobody between you and the goalie. One on one, baby!

> **Proper Coach's Commentary:** "Don't shoot too early!"
>
> **Opposing Parent Psycho Heckle:** "MISS! MISS! MISS!"

SCREEN: When somebody blocks the goaltender's view so he can't see the puck.

> **Proper Coach's Commentary:** "Don't wait too long to shoot!"
>
> **Opposing Parent Psycho Heckle:** "Hey! That bum's in the crease!"

HAT TRICK: When somebody scores three goals in a single game.

> **Proper Coach's Commentary:** "Give that man a contract!"
>
> **Opposing Parent Psycho Heckle:** "Hey! That bum's in the crease again!"

Time-Out: FIGHTING

Sure, fighting is part of hockey. Usually when the pros engage in an exchange, there's a weird protocol. The gloves are dropped. The punchers square up, fists high, and it literally looks like boxing on skates. Somebody throws a punch, somebody gets in close, somebody pulls somebody's jersey over his head, and the refs just watch—until, of course, the players drop to the ice and began wrestling around as they lay on the surface of the rink. That's when the zebras step in and separate the sluggers. Both men are picked up, brushed off, and then sent to the penalty box for a little five-minute nap. Five for fighting.

A long list of rules and regulations for youth hockey absolutely forbids out-and-out brawling (or "fisticuffs," as the folks at USA Hockey quaintly describe it), but the occasional rap in the facemask usually goes unpenalized. Ollie and his defensive colleagues were given explicit instructions to protect their goalie *at all times*, especially after a whistle. This led to some pretty open hostility between Ollie and forwards from the opposing team during any given game.

Here's what usually transpired: Ollie would spend about a third of his time on ice "tying up the shooter." The opposition would send a man to hang around in front of the net and wait for a pass that he could smack into the goal. Ollie would get his shoulder into the kid's back, place his stick under the enemy's stick, and pull up. This kept the bad guy off balance and the bad guy's stick off the ice, which made for a situation where the bad guy couldn't accurately shoot the puck.

If the other defenseman covered the potential shooter, it was Ollie's job to play another guy. Inevitably the puck would wind up by the boards in the corner—where the rink curves on either side of the net—and Ollie would go after the offensive player who was trying to pass the puck to the guy by the goal. It was perfectly legal for Ollie to pin the guy up against the glass, and Ollie never shirked from the assignment.

This, of course, led to some pretty furious forwards on the opposing team. In any sport, a good defense is designed to frustrate the hell out of an opponent. In hockey, you express your frustration openly. The whole thing would come to a head when an enemy shooter would keep whacking away at a prone goaltender who'd already covered the puck. Pissed at being robbed of his victory lap, the forward in question would try to pry the puck loose from the goalie's grip. Ollie would shove the guy off his netminder by any means necessary. He'd use his gloves or his stick or his shoulder, and the kid he was tangling with usually got the worst of it.

Behavior like this almost never led to a roughing call, especially if an overzealous forward was hammering away at the goalie even after the ref had whistled the play dead. The forward would scramble to his feet, look at Ollie (who was inevitably staring at the kid like he'd just committed a double murder), and throw a punch at Ollie's facemask.

Amazingly, Ollie never seemed to retaliate.

The same kid who would scream and complain and carry on about picking up his room, hauling his clothes to the laundry room, or taking the dog out into the yard with him would gladly take a left jab from some punk wearing a Cyclones jersey. Oliver would duck back, cushioning the force of the punch, and wait for the ref to raise a hand and lead the enemy over to the box. Two minutes for roughing.

Ollie never broke eye contact. The kid always kept his vision locked solidly on the eyes of his opponent. The two would glare at one another, Oliver drifting a little in front of the net, the other kid shuffling off to the box with his head turned back to stare down number seventy-four. Sometimes Oliver would mumble something or other that might have been considered a taunt if not for his careful phrasing: "Thanks for the power play, Cincy!" or "Time to catch your breath, there, dude."

Oliver's restraint frightened me just a little. The kid was waiting. Waiting for next year, when he was really, honestly, legally allowed to do some serious hitting.

One Sunday morning I opened the sports page of our local rag. The *Indianapolis Star* featured a daily sports quote on the second page of the section. This day I was met with the affable gaze of a neckless NHL defenseman named Chris McAllister. He'd just been traded to the Colorado Avalanche in a deal with Philadelphia's major league squad. Chris told the press: "My job is to beat the crap out of anyone who hits Peter Forsberg."

Most good NHL teams throughout the history of the league have had their stars, their scorers, their golden boys—Gretzky being the most obnoxious example. They've also had their thugs. Goons. Cement heads. It has always been the role of the thugs to let the Gretzkys skate free, fearless, and unconcerned. The thugs make their presence known early in a season or early in their tenure with the team: Touch Wayne and it's time for lights out. Lay a finger on The Great One and I'll come in low when you're by the boards—and I'll be gunning for your knees. Like playing hockey? Don't smack Ninety-nine. If you do, I just might end your career.

The NHL games got a bad rap for all of the aggression. The casual fan didn't seem to focus on what allowed the greats to set their records. For every uninjured sniper there was a grinning ape like McAllister, ready to step in and intimidate the opposition: Don't touch our moneymaker—he won't be gunning for revenge, but I will.

Ollie liked Gretzky, but he *really* liked McAllister.

I had another vision, a flash forward into a rink in a city with a pro team. Was I watching Ollie play in Fort Wayne? Had he made it to Detroit? No matter. Major or minor, the guy next to me had the same complaint: "Hey! Seventy-four! When's your next parole hearing?"

RESUME PLAY

In late February I went to New York to cover the Grammy

Awards for my radio station and Indy's local CBS-TV affiliate. That particular year the Grammy Awards had moved from Los Angeles to the Big Apple. I went with Dave O'Brien, my partner on our radio show. We had credentials that gave us access to the red carpet outside the awards, and we brought tuxedos for the event.

While I was spending the weekend doing interviews and bumping shoulders with pop stars at Madison Square Garden, Amy and Oliver were getting ready to go south for a three-game stand against the Evansville Thunder. They hitched a ride with Coach Mac and bunked with a fellow player's relatives down in the southwestern corner of the state. (I couldn't think of two places more divergent; Evansville seemed to be a 180-degree shift from New York City.)

Saturday night, the kids went to bed early, and the adults spent the night getting good and shellacked. The next morning, the Ice began pummeling the squad from Evansville while Coach Mac and the rest of his accomplices nursed hangovers of varying degrees. A hangover is something you definitely don't want to be dealing with in an ice rink, even when it's quiet. It's bright and cold, and the highest frequencies of every sound are amplified tenfold. Add buzzers, whistles, and a stand of yelling parents, mix in some Zamboni exhaust, and you've got that bottom circle of hell that even Faust himself couldn't have imagined.

The Indy Junior Ice Squirt A Travel Hockey team won both games against the Evansville Thunder. The caravan from Indy dragged itself back home through the snow on Sunday night.

I flew back to Indy on Monday afternoon. The schedule I'd kept in New York had left me gassed; I spent two days trying to grab as much sleep as I could. The Ice had a make-up game against Columbus, Indiana, on Wednesday, and I wanted to see the team again after missing a weekend. Most of the hockey parents were becoming more and more satisfied with the team's level of play; the kids had started to really gel after Coach Mac's lecture. Games that had been lost by a goal were now being won by that same thin margin. The kids passed to one another readily and really tried to work together.

More important, though, the kids had forgotten how to quit.

Early in the season, if the Ice got behind by two or three goals, the game was essentially over no matter how much time was left on the clock. Their shoulders would slump, the speed would leave their skates. It was simply a matter of waiting for the buzzer to sound.

Not anymore. The kids were skating at top speed for three twelve-minute periods. No rest. No comfort. No quarter for the enemy. Up two goals? Try and go up four. Down three? Pick up the pace.

I strolled into Pan Am Plaza right after leaving my office on the Wednesday after the Grammies. Ollie and his crew were skating like madmen. They went up on the Columbus Flames early and never lost the lead. Of course, every hockey parent wanted to grill me about all the famous people I'd seen in New York, but in between the names I was dropping, I did manage to hoot for the Ollie and his teammates. To be sure, I wasn't alone.

There was a hockey mom who, throughout the course of the season, had developed a reputation as being the Loudest Human Being on the Planet. Most of her commentary was directed at her boy, whom we'll call "Junior" for the time being. Mom's remarks were limited to three basic commands:

"SKATE, JUNIOR, SKATE!"

"JUNIOR! GET IN THE GAME!"

"IF THEY AIN'T GONNA CALL IT, GO AHEAD AND HIT SOMEBODY!"

Of the three, the first was by far her constant standby. It was the directive uttered most often by the mom in question.

Since a few choice parents were busting up in laughter every time the mom in question uttered a shout, I realized I'd missed a pretty good joke or two while the team was in Evansville and I was in New York. Fortunately, my wife cracked pretty easily.

"We found out that (Mom in Question) wanted to sign up (Junior) for singing lessons. We were wondering how *that* would've sounded."

I grinned. "SING, JUNIOR, SING!" I squeaked, just loud enough for Amy to hear.

The rest of the parents, of course, had run through every possible scenario. Junior in math class: "CARRY THE ONE, JUNIOR!" Junior's first date: "GET YOUR TONGUE IN THE GAME, JUNIOR!"

The mom in question could be distracting, but, as I mentioned, she yelled only at her own child. It simply wasn't kosher to heckle the ten-year-old offspring of somebody else.

Right?

MARCH—1st PERIOD

Tournament hockey at the youth level is akin to playoffs in the colleges and pros. Everybody gets in, but the teams are seeded in brackets based on their win/loss record. If a division of the tourney includes ten teams at one age level (Squirt) who are at the same skill level (A), then the Squirt A team that finished first in the regular season will start the tourney against the worst Squirt A team. The second-place team plays the next-to-last team, and so on.

Tournament hockey brings out the best in the kids playing hockey and the worst in the parents watching hockey. Moms wear boas made of fringes of felt in the team's colors and shake clear plastic bottles full of beads of those same colors. Dads wear caps and fleeces complete with professional duplicates of the kid's team logo. This gives everybody the right to scream and yell and carry on like miscreants, grousing at ref and kid and coach alike.

The moms and dads who are living through their children are truly exposed during tourney time. They want their children to have that small glimmering shred of fame that they can only vaguely remember or never even had for themselves. Winners get tribute from the league. Winners are immortalized in brass and emulsion and cheap newsprint.

Win, and your name will adorn a plaque screwed into the wooden base of a cheap cup displayed for all the world to see in the trophy case of your team's home rink. The kids will be photographed, lying on the ice around the trophy, sweaty with hair disheveled from their helmets, grinning and giving the thumbs-up sign or the devil-horns sign or, on occasion, the finger. The photo will be displayed next to the trophy and then reprinted in regional hockey newsletters and small-town newspapers. It's only after the photograph is reproduced several thousand times in all its grainy glory that somebody will notice that one of the kids is flipping off the camera.

The Buckeye Youth Travel Hockey Tournament was held in Cincinnati, Ohio, during the first weekend in March. Oliver's team, after its winning streak against Columbus and Evansville, was seeded seventh in a field of ten. The Ice would play a team from Ohio that they hadn't faced all year, the Dayton Gems.

The Buckeye league was cut into two divisions: One drew from Indiana and western Ohio; the other included mostly central Ohio teams. The central division included the Gems, a bunch of kids who had the misfortune to wear a giant picture of what looked like an engagement diamond on their jerseys.

The tourney was slated for the annex of the Cincinnati Gardens. The Gardens was the home of a minor-league team called the Cincinnati Mighty Ducks (KILL EMILIO KILL EMILIO KILL EMILIO).

The opening game for the Junior Ice faced off at one o'clock on a Friday afternoon. I flew out of work at eleven o'clock and found myself pushing eighty miles per hour on I-74. The day was cloudy and cold.

Ollie and Amy had ditched school and work and taken a ride to Cincy with Jenny and her son, Jeremy. The kids were excited. It was tournament time—the playoff season.

I pulled off the interstate and drove down Seymour Avenue. I wheeled my Saturn through a neighborhood full of graffiti. The rink was wedged among acres and acres of abandoned public housing, a viable venue operating in a city full of plywood windows. The homes that were occupied seemed to house poor African-American families. The building's immediate neighbors were a liquor store covered with wrought-iron security grates and a radiator shop with a hand-painted sign. Here, in the middle of the ghetto, came an army of parents and children ready to take part in a horribly expensive sport that was almost exclusively caucasian. My car skidded into the parking lot outside the Cincinnati Gardens, sliding a bit on the ice left from the last snowfall. I bounded past the main building. A handwritten sign taped to the glass of the box office directed me to the annex next door.

The Cincinnati Gardens? I could see nary a plant within five hundred yards of the venue. An old woman struggled up the sidewalk in front of the Gardens, pulling a cart full of groceries behind her through the cold. I sprinted into the annex. The head of a Mighty Duck grinned at me; a plywood logo hung on the masonry wall just to the right of the doors of the annex (KILL EMILIO!).

I was late. The game had already started and was four minutes into the first period with a 0–0 score on the board. If the kids won this game, they could continue their march toward a Buckeye League Championship. Lose, and they'd be kicked into the "consolation" bracket. Since every team was promised two games but the tourney's rules demanded single-elimination for the big marbles, the notion of the consolation bracket ensured that every parent got her money's worth.

The annex was another grim industrial-looking building with a cold concrete floor. So many of the rinks Ollie played in could've doubled as airplane hangars, and this one wasn't any different. The vaulted ceiling above me was covered with some kind of white-surfaced insulation that had been stuffed between the exposed steel beams, and the stuff had started to come down. Parts of the ceiling looked like somebody's attempt to duplicate the look of a limestone cave filled with stalactites.

On the upside, the place was bright, the boards were sturdy, and the glass was clear. Aluminum bleachers sat at one short end of the rink. A counter had been stocked with sweatshirts that read "Hockey Mom" or "Hockey Dad" or even "Hockey Grandma." Nobody seemed to be buying the "Hockey Grandma" items.

An item that *was* selling: Mardi Gras beads. Amy seemed to have about a dozen around her neck. I slid up to her and whispered, "Who saw your boobs?"

"Nobody yet," she giggled.

I had—and have—a wife who likes sports a little and likes sex a bunch. I am truly blessed.

I also had—and have—a son who plays hockey. I am an emotional wreck and a financial basket case.

My opinion of Ollie's true abilities had morphed continuously during the season. A graph of my confidence in the kid's skills would've looked like the Tilt-A-Whirl at the state fair. Some weeks I thought the boy was a brilliant player who made up for speed with his brain. Other weeks I thought that Ollie was the slowest kid on skates, and nothing more.

No matter how I felt about Oliver's game, though, I prided myself on having learned to keep my mouth shut beyond the grand generalities of "Attaboy!" and "Think!" Coach Mac had told me once: "These kids get home and their dads start tellin' 'em what to do. It's always the goddamn opposite of what I'm tellin' 'em to do. So I gotta ask 'em: Is your old man on the bench? Did he tell ya how you're gonna score against that goalie or who we gotta double-team? Nope. For an hour, I'm the boss. Ignore your mom's yellin'. Ignore your dad's screamin'. We got us a game to win. I'm your coach. I'll help ya win it."

Eventually, my attitude flattened out: Ollie had some talent, a tremendous drive, and a passion for ice hockey. The coaches loved the fact that he made eye contact when they spoke to him. He was attentive. He wanted to learn. And he'd learned a lot over the course of the season.

The player I saw in Cincy wasn't hesitant or tentative. He was aggressive, but not violent. He knew his position, he played it right, and he lived for the moment when he could shove somebody off of Matt, the goalie: "Coach said if anybody goes after Matt, I'm allowed to knock him on his ass!"

We thought the kid had been bragging. Amy had noticed that Ollie's threat was something more: It was a mantra. The kid had said it at least a dozen times during the ride to Cincy. Amy had realized that Ollie psyched himself up by repeating: "Coach said if anybody goes after Matt, I'm allowed to knock him on his ass!"

He was Agent 0074 with a license to kill.

Amy and I watched Ollie race up and down the ice. The score stayed knotted until the end of the second period, when a Columbus forward knocked in a wicked shot from a very wide angle. The puck came in high—Matt didn't have a chance at it.

The Ice had been effective, though—everyone had taken a crack at the Columbus net. Jared, Cody, Taz, Christian, Amanda, John Michael, Dan—every single offensive player, one after another, had seen a clear shot at the net and taken it. Our team was playing brilliant hockey. Absolutely nothing could beat them. Nothing except ...

A really hot goalie.

Time-Out: GOALIES

Pity the poor child swimming in pads in front of the net, the poor kid who lies on his belly, back arced in some kind of ersatz yoga pose while Mom laces up the giant pads that protect his shins and thighs, the poor child with the oversize stick upon whom an entire game can depend.

It's bad enough during the regular season, but goalies can really suffer during tournament time. Some tournaments are set up on a point system: A team will receive one point for every period won, two points for winning a game, zero points for losing, and a single point for a tie. Youth hockey games usually don't go into overtime, so a tie is a fairly common result.

Unless, of course, the tourney is based on a strict win/loss record. In that case, there's no overtime—there's a shootout.

Your five best men line up on the bench. Your first shooter takes the puck from the center line. The goalie can't come out of the crease until the shooter makes contact with the puck. After that, it's very nearly a guessing game for the man in net. Will the shooter go high, low, left, right, what?

Then it's the other team's turn to fire at your goalie. Best of five wins. Tied after five shots apiece? Line up your next five players and go another round.

That's a hell of a lot of pressure for a grown man—and an absolutely spirit-crushing experience for a ten-year-old boy.

Pity the poor goalie who lets that winning shot in. Shootout or not, the goalie who lets the Big One go by always seems to act the same way: frozen and prone, knees on the ice, head down, as if he's converted to Islam and is facing Mecca to offer his devotion to Allah.

Goalies are like baseball pitchers. A goalie on a hot streak is as unbeatable as Roger Clemens in his prime—when a goalie gets it in his mind that he will arrive at a point in space prior to the puck, he will *not* be scored upon. But a goalie who is watching the biscuit slide by him regularly can fall apart—and a goalie whose confidence has been shattered will miss everything that comes his way.

RESUME PLAY

The goalie from Dayton was a machine during the first game of the Buckeye tourney. The kid stopped everything. He stopped pucks that came in top shelf (top of the net, that is), midsection, low in the corners, and in the five hole (between the legs). Everything got blocked. Wave after wave of purple madmen fired at the kid, and only a single disc managed to dribble through, a weird caroming thing that bounced off of three players before sliding slowly over the goal line.

For their part, our goalie and defense—Ollie, Jeremy, Freddy, and Patrick—did a great job. The Gems were held to just two goals.

It didn't matter. The final buzzer sounded with the score Gems 2, Ice 1.

The championship was gone. (Not that the Ice had a shot, mind you—most folks knew that the Buckeye tourney would simply be a coronation ceremony for the big, fast Butler County

Blackhawks.) The Junior Ice would return to the Gardens later that night for a matchup with the Evansville Thunder. It was time for the kids to eat pizza, time for Mom and Pop to drain a beer and share their money troubles with all the other hockey parents. It was time to check into one more Marriott and ice down the cooler one more time. The consolation bracket's final matchup was scheduled for eight o'clock Sunday morning. If the Ice made a habit of winning from this point forward, we were all going to have a fat hotel bill.

Time-Out: HOTELS

Usually the hotels were kind enough to hold rooms for us with the understanding that our entire group would bail on the second night's reservation if the tourney went south for our tykes. We always reserved blocks of rooms as a group, granting us cut rates wherever we stayed. Since all of our non-smoking mansions—including two king-sized beds and a mini-fridge, microwave, and coffeepot—were reserved at the same time, names were meaningless. I was once addressed with, "And how many nights are you staying, Mr. Ice?" On the bright side, at least no hotel desk clerk ever called me Mr. Squirt.

Check in. Lug your junk to the room. Pool's that way, next to the elliptical trainer and combination Universal/Nautilus weight thing that's gathering dust. Scout it out. The hot tub is already full of eight-year-old travel soccer players from Toledo. One of them is standing in the middle of the hot tub, eyes half closed, faint grin: Make a mental note that the hot tub may be contaminated with eight-year-old travel soccer pee. Advise fellow parents and hockey children.

Return to room. Pull beer from cooler, put into fridge. Fridge seems warmer and stinkier than eight-year-old travel soccer pee. Put beer back into cooler. Check microwave. Microwave has one setting: Pompeii. Wonderful for burning popcorn and turning frozen pizza bagels into Goodyear radials. Coffeepot—turns on and off. Plenty of bagged-in-the-filter four-cup coffee bean packs. Can't figure out which one's decaf. Typeface too small. Mental note: Need new glasses.

Pull comforters off beds. Those comforters—yeesh. I've seen the TV reports with the black lights ...

TV—where's the remote? The remote—ah, it's been bolted to the nightstand. At a hotel this expensive? TV—works! Check! What's this? *Stewardess School* is on Spectravision? Man, if the kids weren't here ...

RESUME PLAY

Oliver's team had been thumping Evansville all year, and the Friday-night game against the Thunder looked to be a repeat. The Ice hit three quick goals early, and it wasn't until the second period that Evansville started acting like a hockey team.

The Cincy refs were letting the kids hit a good bit as well; the shots these preadolescents were dishing out to one another had every parent in the rink gasping at times. It was tournament hockey, and the refs didn't want to settle a game with a single call.

Early in the third period Evansville put itself on the board with a goal. Four minutes later the Thunder put another one in. With less than two minutes left in the game, Cody went into the penalty box for tripping. Now Evansville would finish out the game with a one-man advantage.

We thought.

A tremendous hit from behind landed Jared in the box as well, with fifty-seven seconds left in the game. The Ice would have three men in the rink (plus Matt) while the Thunder would pull their goalie so as to have six shooters attacking our squad. The rink was deadly quiet as shot after shot was slapped toward Matt—he kicked a puck here, slapped one away with his stick there, batted pucks away from the net with his glove over and over and over again. An Evansville winger snatched a long rebound before it crossed the blue line and skated directly toward the Ice's net.

The clock ran—5,4,3—the Evansville player juked left, then right, then got in close, ready to shoot—

And the buzzer sounded. He'd waited too long. As he pumped his arms through the motion of a solid wrist shot, the timer expired. The puck slid into the net after the clock read zeroes—no goal.

The teams lined up to shake hands. I drifted over to a bulletin board that had the brackets posted to see who we'd play next. On Saturday afternoon, the Ice had a date with the Cincinnati Cyclones. We headed for our hotel, where the kids were hoping to unwind with a spirited round of knee hockey.

Time-Out: KNEE HOCKEY

Knee hockey is a hotel manager's worst nightmare. Knee hockey is a game played with plastic sticks that are two feet long and a goal of roughly the same height. The goal is constructed from PVC piping and a net, and the scoring object is a foam rubber puck or ball. The game is played by children staggering around on their knees in hotel hallways or conference rooms. The rules seem to be as follows: Put the puck or ball into the net. If you can't, crack your stick against the knuckles of everybody else who's playing. Tackling is allowed. You get extra points for screaming at the top of your lungs. The winner is the team with the most points when the hotel manager tells you all to stop or, by God, he'll throw the entire team, parents included, out into the street at nine o'clock on a frozen Saturday night.

Knee hockey is what the kids do when the parents are gossiping about one another. Who's been drinking? Who never will? Who's flirting with everybody? Who's too much of a prude? Who's sick? Who's tired? Who's sick and tired? Who's got fake boobs? Who's taking Prozac? Who was in the hot tub by the pool with the assistant coach and that weird guy from Dayton when her husband couldn't come to the tournament?

Our hotel in Cincinnati had outlawed knee hockey. A five-minute game in the halls of the brand-new Marriott where the Ice was camping out resulted in a swift and panic-stricken visit from the manager on duty. He'd been extremely concerned about giant gashes in the dark wooden molding and the sheetrock around it. We calmed the manager's nerves and promised that our kids would behave. The adults were another matter entirely.

MARCH—2nd PERIOD

Banned from knee hockey, some of the kids in our group immediately went for a swim in the hotel pool. Okay, maybe not a swim so much as a wildly dangerous wrestling match in the shallow end. The kids had put together some kind of strange football game in which one player was forced to stagger from one side of the pool to the other while maintaining possession of a spongy football that had been ripped in half. Of course, the true object of the contest for everybody else in the pool was to drag the ball carrier under the surface. The game ended when Jared emerged from the pool with red, watery eyes and an egg-shaped knot on his forehead. A defensive player had tackled the kid way too close to edge of the pool.

A mother from our group appeared and admonished the dads who'd been poolside. "Weren't you watching them?" she exclaimed as Jared trundled out of the pool area, holding his head and sobbing.

The dads shrugged. Yeah, we had been watching.

But what were we watching? Watching the kids violate the

third rule on the sign on the wall by the pool, No Horseplay? What's horseplay, anyway? Surely a game of fourteen-on-one-tackle-pool-half-football didn't count as horseplay, did it? No one was fed carrots for running around a dirt track or given sugar cubes for counting with his hooves. No one dragged a beer wagon through St. Louis or whinnied and bucked to try to throw a cowboy so he'd break his collarbone. No horseplay here.

The dads had been watching. And commenting on the intricacies of fourteen-on-one-tackle-pool-half-football. And we'd all seen Jared crack his head against the side of the pool. Well, to be accurate, we'd heard it. To be totally honest, we were talking about hockey just then and ignoring the kids entirely.

This is something that drives my wife absolutely nuts. I've heard her, on more than one occasion, utter something to the effect of: *"You saw the game. Why do you have to spend the next six hours reliving it?"*

Six hours. Ahh, the poor, deluded woman. Any guy worth his weight in jockstraps knows that you don't spend hours re-living the great glories and bitter defeats of your favorite team—you spend a *lifetime* reliving them.

Time-Out: NOT-SO-INSTANT REPLAY

Why does NFL Films exist? Or ESPN Classic? We all know how those games end. We've seen the last chapter—*and* the first kickoff or tip-off or face-off, *and* all the stuff in the middle. Those moments, proud or painful, are etched into our brains forever. It's the way American guys are wired.

Here's my personal rundown of Stuff That Occupies My

Frontal Lobes in the Parts that Don't Think About Sex, Food, Sex, Beer, Sex, Money, Sex, and Sex:

Peyton Manning breaks Marino's single-season touchdown record, and Ollie and I saw catch number forty-seven live in Indy … It's 1979, and I'm in the stands when the Pirates take the last game from the Orioles to win the World Series … Syracuse gets beat by Indiana University with Keith Smart's last-second hoop (did I mention I went to Syracuse University?) … Ollie's tournament slap shot with a broken hand … Scott Norwood—the Bills—WIDE RIGHT WIDE RIGHT WIDE RIGHT (did I mention I went to Syracuse University?) … The Indiana Pacers' Reggie Miller beats the Knicks in the playoffs with a clutch three-pointer that makes Spike Lee's jaw hit the floor … Ollie's first hip-check that flipped a kid … Syracuse and Carmelo Anthony finally take the NCAA Basketball Championship … Syracuse football goes 11–0 in the regular season only to emerge from the Sugar Bowl with a tie when Auburn Coach Pat Dye has his team attempt a field goal as time expires instead of going for the win (did I mention I went to Syracuse University?) … The Colts come back against the Tampa Bay Buccaneers for a win on Monday Night Football … Ollie's Mite team wins a championship game at Ellenberger … Ollie's Mite team wins a championship game at Ellenberger … Ollie's Mite team wins a championship game at Ellenberger …

Every one of these moments is drawn like a Da Vinci charcoal on the surface of my forebrain. I can tell you each and every detail of those moments—the sounds, the smells, the charge, and the trauma of rooting for the team. You can multiply that charge geometrically when it's your kid out there. You'll suffer when he does, cheer when he scores—times a hundred, times a million—you, dear Dad, are the ultimate empathy, a lightning rod for emotion. If you've ever uttered the words "I'm feelin' ya, kiddo," you know it is not a hollow phrase. It's a fact. Your son's stress is your stress. His pain is shared. You both glance nervously at the clock when the team is one goal ahead with three minutes left. Alas, your heart is older and in greater danger from all the lousy drive-thru slop you've ingested, but you are right there with your boy. And when his team wins ...

And when his team wins, you want to tell the world: "That's mine out there. I made that one." That little player full of heart and guts, the tiny bugger who flunked his Social Studies test but still managed to help the squad beat Dem Bums from Someplace Else—that's your boy.

And when another Dad strolls by and mentions: "Hey, ol' Ollie sure played a helluva game," you don't answer out loud. You smile and nod. You don't want to appear like you're living that moment through your child. But you are. You are. Be honest. The voice in your head has a response.

"Hey, ol' Ollie sure played a helluva game."

"Yeah—that's cause *I* made him. That's right! That's my *BOY*, dammit! Right here [pointing to crotch], *that's* where he came from! That's *my* little bundle of talent and genius and skill that *I* delivered into the world for *your* benefit, kind sir!"

Mom, of course, would ask you who exactly squeezed the little bundle of talent and genius and skill through her pelvis after all the puking, belly fat, and backaches, thank you very much. Now shut up and sit down.

RESUME PLAY

Coach had called a curfew. The kids were sawing logs by 10 p.m. Most of the parents followed suit, save for a few die-hards—

primarily coaches, mind you—who felt the need to empty the hotel bar of all of its light beer. At about 1 a.m., a fight broke out between two members of the Columbus Flames Pee Wee coaching staff. After a brew or two or thirteen, the two had begun jawing at one another about the best strategy to use in their next game. Coach Mac, friends with both of the coaches, had been egging the two men on.

"You gonna take that kinda mouth from him?" Mac asked one. He'd wait for a response and then tell the other, "Ha! He sure put you in yer place!"

The hockey debate led to swearing, the swearing led to a remark about somebody's mother, and the remark led to punching. The fight started at one end of the sixth floor hallway, the same floor where every member of the Junior Ice Squirt A team was quartered. The two coaches somehow got themselves into a clinch and slammed repeatedly into the door of a room occupied by Hockey Mom Dee and her son Tyler. Dee and Tyler locked themselves in the bathroom, crawled into the tub, and called the police on Dee's cell phone. The cops, although fairly amused by the bloody condition of the two now-shirtless boxers, issued the two men a stern warning. The two fighters didn't want to press charges against one another, and the hotel didn't want a brawl in the hall turning up in the local newspapers, so the authorities decided that a lecture for the coaches was punishment enough.

(Both coaches spent the next day's game at opposite ends of the Columbus bench, too embarrassed to make eye contact with one another. Despite the distractions, Columbus won anyway.)

Most of the Junior Ice team and its moms and dads slept through the altercation. Saturday dawned cold and cloudy. The coach asked all the kids to gather in the hotel dining room for a pep talk and a little warm-up.

"Okay," said Mike, "laps around the hotel!"

The kids stared in disbelief.

"Did ya hear me?"

Mike led his squadron of bed-headed preadolescent hockey players through the front doors of the hotel, and for the next fifteen minutes the kids ran clear around the building. Mike stood in the parking lot, clapping and slapping the kids on the back as they jogged past him.

When the coach decided that the boys had run enough, he pulled them back into the dining room. Some sat down immediately, a few bent forward and put their hands on the knees, and two of the most winded laid right down on the carpet.

"Good start to the day, guys!" Mike gestured toward the breakfast buffet line. "And today I made sure there are enough donuts for everybody!"

Donuts? Okay, so Mike wasn't a proponent of a *real* strict training regimen, but ... donuts?

Five minutes later, there weren't any donuts left on the breakfast buffet.

We wiped the chocolate frosting and the powdered sugar from the faces of our tiny Olympians. We jammed all of their stinky gear back into their big stinky hockey bags. We checked out—just in case we lost—but made reservations for Saturday night—just in case we won.

We drove through the plywood ghetto back to the Cincinnati Gardens. As Oliver pulled his hockey bag past the main structure, I noticed the sculptures that adorned the brick building. They portrayed the 1950s idea of modern, highly stylized images of a hockey player, a hoops player, and a man running track. All the sculptures had blank, bland features and the same haircut, and all of them seemed to represent white guys. White folks were using the parking lots. White folks were scurrying in and out of the doors. The Gardens and its population looked as if it had been picked up from an American suburb in 1959 and deposited in the middle of Cincy's urban blight.

We were early, so Oliver and Amy and I wandered away from the annex where the Squirts would play and through a gloomy tunnel to the main building. The Gardens stretched out around us. A high school hockey game was just getting underway. I looked at the banners that adorned the walls. The Cincinnati Mighty Ducks (KILL EMILIO KILL EMILIO KILL EMILIO) played teams like the Syracuse Crunch and the Manitoba Moose, the Providence Bruins (whose logo mirrored its Boston parent team in the NHL) and the Hershey Bears. Originally, the Bears had been named the Hershey Bars (Get it?), but somebody somewhere decided that the name was just too much of a crass commercial pitch. That moniker had been changed decades ago, but apparently this kind of tie-in wasn't a problem anymore— after all, the Ducks of both Anaheim and Cincy got their name from a Disney movie.

We watched a bit of the game and then made our way back to the annex. Teams were arriving and leaving, and the din of the concrete-and-metal structure coupled with the florescent lights made the place look like some kind of weird bus station that only catered to youth hockey families. Hockey bags and sticks were strewn everywhere. Parents tripped over gear left and right while their kids shot balls of tape into the air with their sticks.

Oliver trudged into the locker room. I laced his skates. He growled at anybody who'd listen. "Coach said if anybody goes after Matt, I'm allowed to knock him on his ass!"

Agent 0074 was primed.

The Ice had lost to the Cincinnati Cyclones four times over

the course of the season, usually by a one-goal margin. The Cyclones knew what to expect: The Ice was a team that started slow, got behind early, and played catch-up in the third period. Usually, the Ice was right in the game for the duration, but more often than not, the Ice came up losing.

The parents around the rink began to chant and pound on the boards as the kids warmed up. The Ice wore dark black-and-purple jerseys; the Cyclones skated in their Germanic red-and-yellow-and-black shirts. The kids began to bang their sticks high against the glass as they skated by the corners in a line. The buzzer sounded, ending the pre-game skate. The kids lined up for the face-off.

The ref dropped the puck.

Jared snatched it and flipped it forward to Cody, who passed to John Michael, who scored. Ice 1, Cyclones 0.

The ref dropped the puck.

The Ice moved toward the goal more slowly this time, passing, setting, waiting—Cody ripped a shot toward the net and the Cincy goalie deflected the puck into Christian's waiting blade. Chris flipped the puck deftly over the sprawling goalie. Ice 2, Cyclones 0.

Two minutes of the first period were over. There were ten minutes left in the first and two more periods left to play.

About halfway through the second period, John Michael took a shot at the net. The puck dribbled back out as the goalie scrambled for it. John Michael, a Cincy defender, and the goalie arrived at the rebounded puck at roughly the same time. John took a shot as the whistle blew, and the defender gave him a shove. John shoved back, and the ref issued John a two-minute roughing penalty.

I did something I'd never yet done: I heckled a ref. "Homer

call!" I hollered from my vantage point near the corner.

A Cincinnati parent standing ten feet to my left announced: "Maybe that'll teach your kids to stop hitting after the f---ing whistle."

There it was. The F-bomb. The Word You're Not Supposed to Say at a Youth Hockey Game. The various euphemisms for "poop" and "butt" slipped out on occasion, and it was fairly common for someone not to abbreviate the exclamation known as "S.O.B." But drop the F-bomb, buddy, and all bets are off. The signs posted around the arena even said:

NOTICE: THIS RINK ENFORCES A ZERO-TOLERANCE POLICY:

1. SPECTATORS SHALL REFRAIN FROM USING PROFANITY AT ALL TIMES ...

I glowered at the opposing dad and raised my hands in the classic "What the hell?" pose. He turned away in disgust.

I wasn't going to say a word. I laughed. Simple. Shrug it off. Don't get angry. I wasn't going to get angry. Amy looked at me. Nope. Smiling. Not angry. Not me.

Halfway through the third period, with the Ice up 5–3 and a play traveling toward Matt in the net, Oliver slid into position in front of the crease. He tangled with a Cincy shooter as another Cyclone shot a puck off to Matt's left. Matt dropped onto the biscuit, and the whistle blew. The Cyclone in front of the net took a late whack at Matt's glove, and Oliver responded by giving the offending sticker a shove. The Cyclone staggered back, nearly falling, while Oliver stood still, stick across his body like a quarterstaff—the kid would get another push from Ollie if he attempted to continue play.

The ref put a hand on Oliver's shoulder and pointed at the Cyclone. "Don't take a shot after the whistle, now," he cautioned the boy from Cincy, "and don't go after a prone goalie when the play's dead." The ref pointed to the near circle to the left of the goal. No foul, no penalty. Face-off.

The Cyclone parents exploded. Oliver had his back to the loudest contingent as he waited for the face-off.

"Seventy-four!" came a scream. "You go back home! You're a horrible player! You thug! You goon! Seventy-four!"

Oliver turned in disbelief, then wrenched his head back toward the face-off. The catcalls continued.

One redheaded woman in particular was yelling at the top of her lungs. "Where's the penalty on that little punk?" she shrieked.

Oliver kept glancing over his shoulder. The kid looked like he was developing some kind of nervous tic. The expression on his face was one of pure disbelief. Was somebody's *mom* yelling like that? The ref dropped the puck.

Five minutes later, the game was over: 5–3, Ice. Our kids threw their gloves in the air. The teams lined up to shake hands. The parents lined up to congratulate and console the children as they skated out of the rink, through one of the doors in the boards and onto the rubber mats that kept skates from meeting concrete.

Well, the parents usually provided encouragement. Today was a different story.

The redheaded lady grabbed Oliver by the shoulder and spun him toward her face. She was obviously the mother of the kid who Ollie had shoved. "You are a horrible little boy! You need to go home and learn how to play like a nice person and not like a little punk!"

Mr. S., Dan's dad, was standing next to her. "Totally uncalled for!" he exclaimed. "That's no way to talk to a child!"

Amy ran over. I was a step behind.

Amy engaged the redheaded woman. A friend of Red had

joined the fray. "Excuse me," said Amy. "Why are you touching my child?"

I stepped toward Amy and Red. Amy held up a hand toward me. I knew the signal. She wanted to handle it. I'd only engage Red in a shouting match.

Red's friend, a skinny, angry-looking woman with close-cropped hair, stepped into the ring. I took another step and decided to open my mouth.

"This is unacceptable!" I intoned. Unacceptable? That was the best I could do? Wow, I really sucked at this hockey-parent-confrontation thing.

Skinny turned toward me. "You're raising a criminal. How do you sleep with yourself at night?"

I looked at her. "Actually, I sleep with my wife. Who do you sleep with?" Ah! Good one. That crack ran off the friend.

Skinny moved away from me and walked toward the Cincy locker room. As I turned, I noticed a coach or a team manager hustling Red away from the fracas. Red was being escorted outside.

As the woman was being led away, my dear, sweet, sensitive wife—my Amy, who hangs duckies and bunnies all over our house every spring; my Amy, who has a flier titled "Symptoms of Inner Peace" stuck to the door of the fridge; my Amy, a Montessori preschool teacher who believes that Martin Luther King Jr. and Mahatma Gandhi were the two greatest men who ever lived—my Amy yelled:

"Hey, lady—this is ICE HOCKEY! Why doncha sign yer kid up for ballet next time?"

I stared at my wife.

She was staring at the door that Red had just been led through.

"Bitch," Amy muttered.

Time-Out: PSYCHOTIC BEHAVIOR

I know what you're thinking. In fact, I know what you've been thinking for the past hundred or so pages: "So, this little dust-up in Cincinnati is all the *real* rage you saw between parental types during an entire season of *youth hockey games*?"

Right. Nobody got killed. Nobody got beaten up. Sorry—you're going to make it all the way through this NASCAR race without a single serious crash. No dads administering fatal beatings to other fathers; no instances of a Psycho Dad reaching over the glass and choking the coach. We got lucky. We didn't have any parents that extreme on our squad, nor did we cross paths with any certifiable head cases on the opposition's sidelines.

Maybe we're nicer here in the Midwest. Maybe folks in Indiana save all their true dementia for the basketball sidelines. Maybe, just maybe, since the average Hoosier doesn't expect his little skater to gain a scholarship to Michigan for ice hockey, we're not emotionally invested enough in the sport to become truly psychotic. Or maybe because fewer kids play hockey out here, the law of averages hasn't quite caught up with us yet.

Pity poor Massachusetts, where every kid seems to play hockey. Pity poor Massachusetts, home to two nationally publicized cases of truly sick rink-side behavior since the turn of the century:

Reading, Massachusetts: Hockey dad Michael Costin encourages his son to slash opposing players; father of another player, Thomas Junta, kills Costin for his unofficial sideline coaching. Junta is found guilty of involuntary manslaughter. (The two kids were on the same team. The events in question happened during a practice scrimmage.)

Hingham, Massachusetts: Hockey dad David Sullivan is accused of attacking his fourteen-year-old son's coach in the locker room. Sullivan said the coach was unfairly critical of his boy, who was said to suffer from Attention Deficit Disorder.

Both events hit the network news close to the beginning of the new millennium. A more recent incident occurred in Toronto, where a forty-seven-year-old hockey dad named Bradley Desrocher became upset when his son's coach benched the boy for missing practice. After berating the coach with little effect, Bradley allegedly reached over the glass and began strangling him until the coach blacked out. It's doubtful that any collegiate or pro scouts were watching the game, since Desrocher's boy was nine years old at the time.

For a while, parental behavior was becoming so volatile that the governing bodies of youth hockey in the United States and Canada began an ad campaign with the slug line: "Relax—It's Just a Game."

The message was delivered in poster form at rinks throughout North America. The images featured plastic "bubble-hockey" players—the kind found in arcade games in which two players move and spin the figurines on metal rods. One photograph showed a plastic parent screaming at a despondent plastic kid, another featured a plastic mom throwing a plastic drink at a plastic referee, and a third depicted two plastic parents beating the polymer chains out of one another.

The campaign was slick and clever, tragic and comic, and very arresting. We saw the posters at all the rinks where Oliver played hockey. And at each rink, the parents who cheered kept cheering, the ones who screamed kept screaming, and the ones who acted really scary kept acting really scary.

Because, you see, you can't advertise the jerkiness out of the jerk. You can't market away the sense of entitlement some parents have after spending all this money and time and tire rubber on the season. Either you're going to have to shame, ban, or legislate certain behavior out of existence—which isn't likely—or you're going to have to live with some of the worst examples of human nature.

The next time you're at work, take a gander at the real knuckleheads in your peer group. Observe the brown-noser, the back-stabber, the office gossip, the lazy long-luncher who covers his butt by delegating everything and spends the company dime surfing the Web for recipes or dirty pictures. Consider all of those nitwits. Now, I ask you, if you hung up a sign that read:

"BE NICE—THERE ARE NO STOCK OPTIONS IN THE AFTERLIFE."

... do you think it would do a damn bit of good?

Nope. The jerks don't really think they're jerks. They'd think *you* were a sentimental bonehead for hanging up such *Chicken-Soup-for-the-Soul*-type drivel. They're just doing their jobs, getting ahead, beating the system—whatever. They're *entitled.*

The screaming hockey dad—veins bulging in his neck and his forehead, spittle flying from his grinding teeth and twisted mouth, cheeks a bright crimson from his deranged fury—paid for this dysfunctional display. He earned it, baby. Go ahead and tell him he's wrong for acting like such an ass. He might just punch you in the teeth for your impudence. The true Psycho Dad firmly believes that he's right—and he's not going to listen to reason, especially if it's presented in giant glossy poster format.

Gaze upon Psycho Hockey Dad. What the hell happened to this guy? If you think that the sport of the rink is the cause, forget it. It's just another outlet, a place where an unbalanced individual can really cut loose. No one's pumping Angry Gas into the arena. Those who are predisposed to wax certifiable somehow think that the rink is the acceptable venue for this particular brand of numbskullery, and that's all there is to it. It's hockey, dammit—but really, it's not too different from anywhere else that Psycho Dad happens to turn up.

Psycho Dad can flip off a cop in traffic with junior in the backseat: He's got someplace to be in a hurry, and the construction roadblock is in his way. Psycho Dad can hurl insult after insult at the neighbor with the dandelions in his yard: That son of a bitch is driving down property values. Psycho Dad sees better than the ref, drills better than the coach, and—here's the real frightening part—plays better than his child.

Psycho Dad might irk, annoy, or even scare the crap out of a coach, parent, or casual observer, but remember: You don't have to live with him. You don't have to hear a litany of your faults, your shortcomings, your inabilities, and your cowardice as the words ring angrily in your ten-year-old ears. There are kids whose parents never cross the line into physical rage, yet still drill screaming insults into the psyches of their own progeny night after night throughout the course of the hockey season, the school year, the ballet lesson—whatever—until the joy of a good slap shot or an A+ or the perfect plié has been driven from the child's soul. Now hockey is just a miserable job, school and dance are just occupations ungoverned by child-labor laws.

The kid gets yelled at. The kid keeps playing. The kid carries dad's rage around like a backpack full of lead. The kid grows up and, more than likely, passes that rage to the next generation, where the burden on self-control gets heavier still. Two, perhaps three generations pass until the inevitable tipping point comes and, finally, the son of the son of the son beats his boy's coach to death for some imperceptible violation of that particular Pschyo Dad's warped code of honor.

So why does sideline violence seem to be on overdrive at youth hockey games in North America? The game is rough, the rink amplifies sound, and fighting has been part of the pro sport for decades. Hence the magnifying glass.

Hey, we all get amped up. When Oliver was on the receiving end of what I though was a cheap shot, I got upset. But I didn't take it out on anyone else's child, parent, or coach. Hockey is hockey, and the sport encourages loud spectator participation. As rational, thinking adults, Amy and I felt we needed to keep the hollering positive. I don't know where Red lay on the generational continuum of crazy, but she had crossed a line: She'd put a hand on someone else's child. And she'd been—correctly—removed from the building.

RESUME PLAY

I honestly couldn't tell if the remainder of the Cincy parents were angry, embarrassed, or a little bit of both. They left the rink quietly and without any confrontations besides the occasional less-than-friendly glance. I smiled at everybody. I wasn't going to lose my cool at a kid's hockey game—especially one that was over.

We checked back into our hotel. Coach Mac dropped by our room to drain a few beers and watch a basketball game on cable. Mac told us that the Buckeye league had had problems with the redheaded woman before. He wanted her banned from all future games. "You can say anything you want. Heckling a bunch a'kids ain't right, but you *are* allowed. Lay a hand on kid, though, and you're gone. I'm filing a complaint."

"Those Cyclone parents were flipping out, " I noted. "They figured we'd roll over, I guess."

"That's it," said Mac. "Them Cincy coaches, too. I was telling

Cody by the bench, 'You can't never panic. Look at them coaches over there. That's how somebody looks when they're panicked.' 'Course, the coaches heard everything I said."

Mac smiled.

The Ice turned in early that Saturday night, parents, kids, and coaches alike. The Junior Ice Squirt A Travel Hockey team had one more game to play in the Buckeye League, and the face-off was scheduled for 8 a.m. It was late in the season, and everyone was running out of stamina, patience, and, most important, money.

Intermission: KILLING TIME

Beers and knee hockey, ESPN and video games, chatter and gossip—all of it whiles away the hours of downtime you faced when you and the kids are stuck in a strange city between games in some hotel by the highway, surrounded by strip malls and chain restaurants.

What to do? Go to the Chicken Wing Hut and watch the kids pump dollar after dollar into some horribly violent zombie-killing video game while you burn your palate with chicken parts drenched in Tabasco? Send the whole ten-year-old crew to the movies with the one or two parents who have either the patience of saints or the brains of a stump? (C'mon—who else would volunteer to wrangle fifteen to twenty prepubescent kids?)

We usually opted for the movies. And to be fair, the parents would usually take turns watching the kids. No one—repeat, no one—was either saintly enough or stupid enough to volunteer to play den mother more than once in a row. And because our disposable income had been completely tied up in sticks, pads, and ice time, Oliver and his buds attended many a bargain-basement cinema in their hockey careers. Ollie and the team saw most major motion pictures about three months after they'd dropped off the top-ten lists for box office sales.

The kids would return from these budget theatres with terrific stories about Adventures in Projectionism.

"For, like, the first ten minutes of the movie, there was, like, a black line through the middle of everything, and the bottom half of the people were on top of the screen, and they'd be talking with their heads on the bottom half!"

"Yeah, until the movie broke and everybody booed."

"We got our two dollars back, though. Hey, dad—can we go to Chicken Wing Hut and play Zombie Mercenary 3 with our movie money?"

J

MARCH—3ʳᵈ PERIOD

The main bracket, the championship nod, had been taken—of course—by the Butler County Blackhawks. As teams were knocked out of the primary bracket, they were slated for play in the consolation bracket. The Ice had been dropped to the consolation bracket early, but our team was now playing for a trophy on a Sunday morning against the Flames from Columbus, Indiana.

Oliver hadn't been rattled at all by the crazy mom from Cincinnati. He laughed the whole thing off. He woke up on Sunday morning chanting: "Coach said if anybody goes after Matt, I'm allowed to knock him on his ass!" The team assembled in the lobby of the hotel, pushing each other at the breakfast bar, grabbing for a bowl of Lucky Charms and a bagel.

We packed the car, checked out of our hotel, and drove through the dark back to the Cincinnati Gardens. The kids assembled in the locker room at 7:15 a.m., silent and determined. The Junior Ice had a mission. These little boys and a single girl were grim-faced. I laced Oliver's skates and left the locker room. I meandered over to the corner of the rink where I'd stood for every single game so far.

The Junior Ice took to the rink and skated in a circle that encompassed half of the playing surface. They hammered their sticks on the glass as they skated past the boards in what had now become a tradition for the team.

The Columbus Flames lined up for the face-off against our kids. The Flames won the opening draw, skated toward Matt, and scored: 1–0.

On the next face-off, the same thing happened: 2–0, Columbus Flames.

Oliver took the ice on the next face-off. The flurry slowed. Oliver and the rest of the defense decided it was time to start bumping people. They did, and they weren't penalized. The defense started hitting people harder. No fouls.

I noticed that the Columbus parents had nary a complaint with the physical nature of this matchup. Their kids were dishing out some pops as well. Still, at the end of the first period, Columbus was up 3–0.

At the beginning of the second, Coach Mike decided to start playing Jared on defense. Jared was one of the fastest skaters on the team and the Ice's leading scorer. Jared took an errant puck that Columbus had tried to send out of their goalie's zone and unleashed a wrist shot toward the center of the ice. The puck slid through as many as four players wearing both Columbus and Indy jerseys before it crossed the goal line. The netminder hadn't been able to see the shot at all—there was quite a crowd blocking his vision.

The drought was over. Our kids were back in it. At the end of the second, the game was tied 3–3. The ref dropped the puck for the last period of the tourney.

Oliver was burned—and to be fair, so was the rest of the defense and the goalie—by a big center for the Flames who blew through the Junior Ice midway through the third. Score: 4–3.

John Michael passed the puck to Jared in front of the Columbus net two minutes later. Shoot, score, and a four-all draw with less than five minutes left.

Hockey is a game of momentum. The emotional swings can generate enough intestinal acid to burn a hole in your stomach quicker than you can spell Yzerman. The score was tied. The game was on the line in the consolation championship match. A bunch of ten-year-olds were battling to exhaustion for third place, and their parents were going nuts.

Columbus and Indy folk beat on the glass and kicked at the boards. I pulled off my Junior Ice ball cap and tossed it aside so I could lace my hands across the back of my skull without interference. Amy was chewing on her nails. Parents were literally jumping up and down as the teams rocketed up and down the ice—shot, save, return, shot, save, return.

Big Flame was lurking behind his goal. Somebody from the Ice fired a shot at the Columbus net. Stick save, loose puck, Big Flame knocked it forward—the puck caromed off of someone's skate and careened back toward Big Flame.

This was his chance. The angle of the rebound had caught the Ice out of position.

Big Flame lurched forward. He crossed the center line as Oliver and Jared both caught up to him. Ollie and Jared both tried to hook the kid, trip him, bring him down, anything, but Big Flame was an irreversible, unstoppable force. Fifteen feet ahead of the Junior Ice crease, Big Flame wound up and fired. The shot went high; Matt guessed low.

Score: Columbus 5, Indy 4.

Columbus had a one-goal lead with a minute-and-a-half remaining. Every time the play drifted away from him, the

Columbus goalie looked up at the clock on the scoreboard. He was experiencing the closest thing any human has ever come to traveling at light speed: Time had slowed to a literal crawl. Einstein himself was running the clock. Every second was a yawning chasm of tension and fear, a terrible grinding of the psyche and a rolling in the stomach. You could see the child taking stock:

Stick down, play's away, now they're back in my zone, be ready, don't come out of the net yet, glove up GLOVE UP that kid's GONNA SHOOT—ah—my defenseman cut him off! Poke check! They cleared the zone! They're moving down toward the other net! How long was— three seconds? All of that only burned THREE seconds off the board?

For the Junior Ice kids, alas, they were still on Earth time. For those on Earth time down by a goal, the stretch between that last point and the final buzzer lasted about as long as it took for dear Professor Albert to snap his fingers.

Ninety seconds later the Buckeye Travel Hockey season ended for the Junior Ice Squirt A team as the awful honk of the buzzer ricocheted off the walls and glass of the rink. When you are losing a hockey game, that last klaxon has a mocking sound. When you win, it's a Handel chorale.

The Columbus kids threw their gloves in the air. They skated over to their goalie and tackled him. Sticks littered the ice.

The kids from Indy leaned on the boards by the bench, watching the celebration. They'd finished the tourney in fourth place out of ten teams after ending the regular season in seventh.

The kids lined up to shake hands and then straggled off the ice. Parents from Columbus and Indy smiled at each other.

"Helluva hockey game, great to watch."

"Your kids played great."

"So did yours."

"Shame they couldn't share that trophy."

"Yep. Damn shame."

Ah, the pleasant attitude of those who have just been granted a reprieve. Gone were the hotel bills and shouting matches, the eggs at Bob Evans and the endless burgers eaten behind the steering wheel, the bills and the fees and the dues and the stupid damned fundraisers that required you to try to sell scented Yankee Candles to your poor, glassy-eyed coworkers. All of it was done until next season.

The weekend would become your domain again, dear Mother and Father of the Puck. Think of it: long afternoons of cold beer and margaritas, ribs sizzling above a tank full of propane as the sprinklers hissed out in the middle of a green lawn. Friends— friends you had not seen since Christmas—friends would darken your door again, bottles of red and white wine in hand, waiting to talk of politics and weather, eateries and automobiles, parties to be planned and adventures to be had—anything but bloody stupid youth hockey.

You and your friends could drag the patio furniture out to the middle of the deck, the deck that stretched into your big backyard, and you could all gaze west into the brilliant Indiana sunset and watch the sky turn blue and purple and black as a thousand fireflies dotted the darkness. Your nose would be filled with the scent of lilacs and honeysuckle and citronella candles—anything but the smoke of a chugging Zamboni or the foul, damp stench of your child's shoulderpads. No buzzers, no boards, no sweatshirts, no ice. Summer, sweet respite, sweet release from the crushing grind of the Youth Travel Hockey Parent.

Of course, as with any addiction, there's always one more hit— the Junior Ice still had a few unofficial games on the schedule.

FINAL BUZZER

Late-season practices—especially as a season is really winding down—can be immensely entertaining for the kids who show up. Every hockey practice Oliver attended after the tourney was a far different experience than the endless drilling and sprinting marathons that had come earlier in the year. The first Tuesday after the tournament saw the Ice Squirts sharing the pad with the Ice Pee Wees.

"Free-for-all scrimmage, big 'uns agin the little 'uns!" hollered Mac. "Check 'em if you like!"

Check them if you like. Number seventy-four had been waiting for those words all his life.

Oliver hit one, then another. He pinned kids to the boards. He slammed kids into the boards. He lowered his shoulder and made a beeline for anybody who looked as if he might end up in the same area code as the puck.

After a few minutes, Ollie's confidence surging, he snatched a puck from a kid on the Pee Wee squad named Darryl. Darryl was not amused, and Darryl skated through Oliver as if Ollie had been nothing more than a cool breeze.

Oliver hit the ice hard and sat. He got up, skated over to the bench, took a drink of water, and then went gunning for Darryl. He lowered his shoulder on the approach. Darryl stopped, turned, and waited. No contest. Oliver looked a lot like a bicycle crashing into a semi. Ollie sat down again.

Later, when I was pulling Ollie's skates off in the locker room, I asked him how he liked it.

"That was great!" he exclaimed. "Did you see me hit those guys? One of the Pee Wees said I was good checker."

"You are," I responded. "Darryl's pretty big, huh?"

"Yeah," he said, "it's gonna take a lot to knock him down."

"Mm-hmm," I murmured. Now I was ready to impart Pearls of Knowledge from the Wise Father. "And what did you learn today, Oliver?" I asked sagely.

Oliver thought for a moment. "I learned that my pants need more padding around the butt."

It's tough to correct logic like that.

The next night the Junior Ice had a rare weeknight double-header in Bloomington, Indiana. Bloomington, known for Indiana University hoops and cycling (remember the movie *Breaking Away?*), wasn't exactly a hotbed of hockey. Still, the town managed to field a few teams every year under the moniker of the Bloomington Blades.

The teams trickled into the rink. It was warm outside, and a lot of kids were wearing shorts as they dragged their gear into the venue. I'd brought my jacket to wear inside the rink.

The Ice went up early on the Blades. After a flurry of goals from the Ice, Coach Mike sent his defensive players out to play offense. Oliver tried to hit a one-timer, a deflection shot off a perfect pass from Jeremy, but the Bloomington goalie got a piece of it. No goal. Not today.

After shutting out the Blades 8–0, the Ice lined up for the second game. This one was tighter, tougher, and more physical. In the third, with the Ice up 2–1, a Blade player took offense to Zack's style of play. As the play moved away from Zack and the Blade player, who were jawing at each other by the Bloomington goal, the Blade suddenly dropped his gloves. Zack's mom could be heard over the din that was erupting: "*He's all yours now, Zachary!*"

For those who haven't heard, the act of dropping the gloves is not a request for a manicure. It is an invitation to stop playing nice and start boxing. Zachary accepted the invitation.

Coach Mike looked at the floor. Coach Mac looked at the floor. Fighting was not allowed in youth hockey. It was called misconduct. Zack would finish the road trip in the locker room.

As it turns out, fighting is also damn ineffective in youth hockey.

Relative to the length of the sport's existence, helmets are a recent addition to the NHL uniform. The modern helmet will protect a player from concussive impacts with the boards, glass, pucks, and sticks, but the player's face is usually an available target when the brawling begins. Gloves get dropped and the punching starts. There's a protocol to it: Fight standing up, and the striped shirts will watch. As soon as the players clinch and drop to the ice, the refs usually break it up. The players are then led to the penalty box, usually bloody from the bare-knuckle contact, to sit and think about playing well with others for five whole minutes. They spit and swear and wipe the crimson from the cuts on their brows, readying themselves for another round.

This cannot happen in youth hockey. In youth hockey, kids wear big metal cages over their faces.

Zack and the Blade threw a total of perhaps four punches before they wheeled away from each other, wincing, whining, and grasping their right knuckles with their left hands. They'd been flailing away at each other's heads—but they might as well have been punching the grates of two Weber grills. Fists hit metal, and the kids were hurting.

I looked at Oliver. He'd been on the bench when the violence started, and now he was leaning over the boards, shaking his head.

The Junior Ice finished the season with a pair of wins. The kids trickled into the locker room and began to pull the pads off and toss them into their bags—some of them for the last time.

Next year—new jerseys, maybe a different number. Maybe a different team. And a bunch of these guys wouldn't even be playing hockey.

It was a sad fact of any sport—hell, any endeavor in life—that some folks fell by the wayside as the demand for more and more skills increased. Some of the kids on the Ice would lose interest in hockey altogether, tired of the early-morning wake-up calls to climb into a set of damp and freezing pads. Other kids would simply be unable to keep up—unable to make the transition to a checking league, unable to take a hit and give it back.

Somebody's pop might get downsized during the off-season. Somebody's folks might get divorced. Somebody might just decide the kid didn't have the chops, didn't enjoy it enough, and the financial hardship was just a little too large. Something might happen, tiny or tragic, that prevented the family from shelling out the massive dough required to let a kid play ice hockey.

Attrition of this kind hits hockey harder than other sports, I think—and especially in those places where it's not an institution. Outside of Michigan or Minnesota, New England, or New York, youth hockey loses a great many kids every year. Many Mites do not become Squirts; many Squirts fail to make Pee Wee; the pool of players is drastically whittled back with each season.

New kids don't seem to enter the league late. The reason is simple: Skating. You don't need to know how to skate to become an offensive lineman for the high school football team. You've heard of collegiate players being proficient at both basketball and football; you've heard of NFL players who could've played baseball—or even played in the majors, like Deion Sanders. But you nearly never hear of an athlete who "also plays hockey for the school."

Hockey seems to consume everything—time, cash, emotion. Hockey is an obsession. An exciting, demanding drug. And not every child can keep up. In fact, most won't.

Some of the kids knew it. Oliver knew it. He stared at his feet as he slowly unlaced his skates. His eyes were wet. He knew that a youth hockey team lasts only for one season. This collection of comrades is fleeting, a five-and-one-half-month collection of personalities and talents. You might be facing off against some of these very same guys come next October. You might never see some of these guys ever again.

Oliver would continue to play. He'd get better every year, climbing through the ranks and being noticed by the coaches scouting talent for next year's travel teams. He'd find himself shooting against the very goalie he'd spent that year protecting. He'd find himself on another bench next to Zack and Tyler. He'd see John Michael with the puck and lay a check on the kid one year, only to be backing him as a defenseman the next.

Oliver would continue to play, but the Junior Ice Squirt A Travel team was finished for the season—and for good.

As we drove out of the Hoosier Uplands and back into the prairie toward Indy, Oliver said little for the first thirty minutes of the ride. After a while, I sensed his mood lightening a bit.

I asked Oliver what he thought of the fight.

"Zack was stupid," he said.

"Really."

"He got thrown out of the game for that. He was punching the guy's facemask. What's up with that? All you do is hurt your fists and you get tossed. That sucks."

The Saturn chugged north as twilight turned to a moonless March night. Winter would soon give way to spring.

It had been a good year. I'd learned how smart and focused Oliver could be. It would be hard for the boy to play the scatterbrain—he wouldn't be shirking off any more parental directions. He had great listening and memorization skills. The coaches had clued me in.

Mike had sent me an e-mail at one point when he'd really been getting a lot of grief from some of the other parents. He wanted me to tell Ollie how glad he was to have him on his team. Ollie helped the younger kids with patience and thoughtfulness. He didn't complain. He just wanted to play hockey as best as he could.

Sure, he'd made mistakes. He'd gotten penalties. He'd wanted a rep as a cement head, a goon, but he didn't have the hole in his conscience that would've actually allowed him to go out onto the ice and really take a cheap shot at another kid. Oliver wasn't that kind of a player.

After the season was over, Ollie had to write a paper for school about what he wanted to be when he grew up. The paper showed me how down to earth the child really was. Ollie wrote that he'd probably become an architect—he loved buildings. (This surprised me a bit.) He did say that he'd make a good hockey coach—how he'd invent skating and shooting drills, how much he enjoyed showing the little kids how to skate or shoot.

He mentioned at the end of the essay that his biggest dream was to play ice hockey professionally. "A coach told me I could be a star in the minors or not so famous in the NHL," he wrote. I didn't ask him what coach had told him that. I didn't know if the coach he referenced had even been telling him the truth. It didn't matter. It made the kid feel good, feel valuable, and that was all I needed to know.

Hockey player? Who cared? I saw the first signs of the kind of man Ollie was becoming. Tough. Conscientious. Kind.

Was it parenting? Was it dumb luck?

Maybe it was good coaching. Maybe it was a combination of all of it. Maybe that unique mix qualifies as dumb luck.

It had been a good year. We'd made some new friends. We'd also seen some folks we'd be sure to avoid the next time we went to Cincinnati.

It had been a good year. The team finished with an overall record of thirty-two wins, twenty-five losses, and three ties. Ollie had led the defense in assists with fifteen. (He'd also led the defense in penalty minutes. He'd made twenty-seven trips to the box. Can't win 'em all.)

It had been a good year. I'd watched some great hockey, and I'd watched some terrific kids gain a little more maturity. All of them, every one, were on the doorstep to adolescence. Ollie had been eyeing the girls since New Year's, and now a good-looking older female practically sent the kid into a seizure. He'd stare and ogle—it bordered on embarrassing.

He was asserting himself as a person. He wore his cap backwards. He listened to hip-hop because everybody else did—and then when skateboard culture invaded his noggin, he devoured every punk song he could get his hands on. He listened to all of it through a set of headphones that was permanently affixed to a personal CD player. Lately, Amy had really begun yelling at Oliver for wearing his pants to low. "I'll ground you for sagging …"

It had been a good year.

We stopped at a convenience store. "Pick out whatever you want," I said. Oliver grabbed a can of Pringles chips and a bottle of chocolate milk. I paid without argument.

"Thanks, Dad!" said Ollie, genuinely surprised that I'd just bought him four dollars worth of horrible junk food. He deserved it.

We got back on Route 37 and headed toward the lights of Indianapolis.

"Still liking hockey?" I asked. "After a whole year of travel and all?"

"Oh, yeah! I'm gonna try out for Pee Wee Double-A Travel next year. That one Pee Wee said I was a good checker." Oliver crunched a handful of chips.

"I wanna go to Michigan," he continued. "I wanna play for the Wolverines. Maybe I'll get to go play for the Red Wings one day. But I'm definitely going to Michigan. That's a good hockey team. Michigan."

"Keep working," I said. "You'll get there."

"Yeah. I'll get a scholarship and play for the Wolverines, and you and Mom can drive up and see all my games."

I rolled down my window a bit. The smell of wet earth drifted into the car. My weekends would now be filled with lawnmowers and seed spreaders. Hockey season was giving way to yard work season.

We turned onto an interstate that dropped us north of midtown. I drove north on Illinois Street toward home and passed the back of the big brick church that faced the Meridian Street corridor, a street lined with old-moneyed mansions and sprawling yards. The sports fields that the church owned were lit up, and we could see a bit of mist hovering just above the baseball diamonds.

Oliver looked out the window at the fields behind the church. "Dad?"

"Yes, Oliver?"

"Can I sign up for Little League next summer?"

Ed Wenck is a radio show host and writer. He lives in Indianapolis with his wife, Amy, his son, Oliver, and two incredibly dumb mongrel mutts, Chessie and Dingo. This is the first time he's tried to pay off his son's hockey expenses by sitting down and writing an entire book.

Books of Interest

For the Hockey Dad Who Becomes a Baseball Dad in the Spring
Baseball Behind the Seams

The **Baseball Behind the Seams** series presents baseball the way it ought to be: no pouting superstars, no steroids, no players' strikes. Each book in this one-of-a-kind series focuses on a single position, exploring it with the kind of depth serious fans crave. Through extensive research, including interviews with hundreds of players past and present, the authors have brought together the most original and informative series ever published on the game.

Each book in the series covers
- The physical and mental qualities of the position
- The position's history
- The plays, and how to make them
- Profiles of the position's top all-time players
- The best defenders of the position
- A day in the life of one player, from arriving at the ball park to the final out
- Lists of Gold Glovers, MVPs, and Rookies of the Year
- Fun and quirky facts about the position

The Catcher	The Starting Pitcher	The First Baseman	The Shortstop
By Rob Trucks	By Rob Trucks	By Tom Keegan	By Rob Trucks
$14.99 Paperback	$14.99 Paperback	$14.95 Paperback	$14.95 Paperback
ISBN: 1-57860-164-9	ISBN: 1-57860-163-0	ISBN: 1-57860-261-0	ISBN: 1-57860-262-9

To order call: 1-800-788-3123, www.emmisbooks.com
Emmis Books, 1700 Madison Road, Cincinnati, Ohio 45206